ELEMENTARY PERSIAN GRAMMAR

BY

L. P. ELWELL-SUTTON

Senior Lecturer in Persian in the
University of Edinburgh

CAMBRIDGE
AT THE UNIVERSITY PRESS
1963

PUBLISHED BY

THE SYNDICS OF THE CAMBRIDGE UNIVERSITY PRESS

Bentley House, 200 Euston Road, London, N.W.1.
American Branch: 32 East 57th Street, New York 22, N.Y.
West African Office: P.O. Box 33, Ibadan, Nigeria

©

CAMBRIDGE UNIVERSITY PRESS

1963

Printed in Great Britain by Stephen Austin and Sons, Ltd., Hertford

TO MY WIFE

for whom this book was
originally written

CONTENTS

vii

INTRODUCTION

The present work is a parallel volume to the author's *Colloquial Persian*, first published in 1941. Whereas the earlier grammar set out to introduce the student to the spoken language only, in this book the aim is to provide a simple but comprehensive framework for the current written language. It is not, however, purely literary in concept, since much modern writing in Persian—in newspapers, novels, short stories, etc.—if not actually colloquial, is decidedly freer in style than the traditional literary forms sanctioned by the classics and still favoured by more conservative writers.

Persian grammar is relatively simple, and the lessons that follow give the essence of all grammatical principles that will be encountered in the course of reading modern Persian books and newspapers. The lessons are also designed, without unduly complicating the student's task, to give him some impression of the characteristic idiom and phraseology of the current language.

The Persian script is introduced in the first lessons, and thereafter no transcription is used (except from time to time to illustrate phonetic points), so that the student is obliged from the start to read in the original script. While this may seem to make the early stages somewhat more laborious, it will be found that, once this initial hurdle has been passed, progress in reading is much more rapid than if, after first learning the language in transcription, the student then had to re-learn it in a different alphabet. It also eliminates the spelling difficulties that arise from the fact that certain sounds—s, z, t, etc.—are represented by more than one Persian letter. Vowelling is fairly complete in the early lessons, and is progressively discarded. All vowels are given in the vocabularies. The script used is the ordinary printed form, but for the benefit of those who wish to proceed further in the reading of letters and other modern manuscripts, appendices are provided on the two written scripts in common use at the present day.

While every effort has been made in the examples and exercises to choose words in common use and of value to the beginner, the selection has not been determined by any statistical examination of newspapers, books, etc. Such counts are often more misleading than helpful, as well as imposing an artificial strait-jacket on the form of the language to be taught. The purpose of the grammar is to familiarize the student with the structure of the language; vocabulary can only be acquired by use, especially in reading, and by conversation where possible. In fact it will be seen that a total vocabulary of about 1,500 words has been used in the book, so that inevitably many useful words have been omitted; but few have been included that are not in common use.

From Lesson VII onwards the exercises take the form of continuous prose passages rather than disconnected sentences. The Persian–English exercises (from Lesson VIII onwards) are taken, with occasional minor modifications necessary to avoid the use of grammatical points not yet treated, from Persian originals; these have been selected for a fairly wide range of literary styles, as well as to illustrate various aspects of Persian life and literature. The English–Persian exercises from Lesson VIII onwards are designed as a 'potted' history of Persia, though emphasis is on linguistic rather than historical requirements.

Although the teaching of spoken Persian is not the primary aim of the present book, a reasonably good intonation and accent in reading is obviously desirable (and also helpful when listening to spoken literary Persian, for example, in radio broadcasts). To this end paragraphs on this point have been included at the end of most lessons, in the form of selections of example sentences already used in the lesson in question, printed in transcription with diacritical points showing approximately the pitch and stress of each syllable. While this is certainly inadequate to teach correct intonation, it will be found helpful in giving some idea of the rhythm of the language, which has a certain bearing on the grammatical and syntactical structure.

My grateful thanks are due to the Carnegie Trust for the Universities of Scotland for the financial assistance which made possible the publication of this book, and to the Syndics of the Cambridge University Press for their most helpful attitude. I would also like to acknowledge assistance given me by Mr P. W. Avery of the University of Cambridge and Mrs Katrina M. Ghafghaichi of Tehran.

LESSON I

The Alphabet

1. The Alphabet

The Persian alphabet, a slightly modified form of the Arabic, consists of thirty-two letters,[1] all primarily used as consonants. Four of these have secondary uses as vowels (see paras. 5, 6, 9 and 21), and there are also three *vowel signs* (see paras. 5, 6, 9) placed over or under the letter that precedes them (but normally omitted in writing or print).

2. The Script

The Persian script is written from right to left, and is cursive, that is to say, the letters of a word are normally joined to one another, even in the printed form.

A few (seven out of the thirty-two) do not join the *following* letter, thus leaving a gap in the word.

There are fifteen basic letter forms, the full number of thirty-two being made up by the use of one or more distinguishing dots over or under the letter and forming an integral part of it.

The shape of each basic form may be further modified by (*a*) a preceding joining stroke, and (except in the case of the seven 'non-joining' letters) (*b*) a following joining stroke, or (when no other letter follows) (*c*) a final tail or flourish.

3. The Nasx Script

There are three styles of writing with which the student will need to become familiar:

> the printed style (*nasx*).[2]
> the copy-book style (*nasta ʔliq*). (See Appendix A.)
> the handwritten style (*šekasté*). (See Appendix B.)

---

[1] For the alphabetical or 'dictionary' order, see para. 30.

[2] For the pronunciation of the sound represented in transcription by the letter 'x', see para. 8; for 'š' see para. 13.

The style to be studied initially is the *nasx*. The other two are derived from this.

All *nasx* letters are tilted slightly forward (in the direction of writing). Four imaginary lines of writing should be visualized, the lowest being the main line of writing, on which the whole of any letter should stand.

4. Group I (One Letter)

Joined to preceding   Separate form   Basic shape
letter only

This letter is not joined to a following letter.

Pronunciation	Joined form	Transcription	Name	Separate form
none	ﺍ...	ʾ	*alef*	ا

Alef stands for the glottal stop (very weak in Persian). It is assumed for the purposes of the Persian script that every word beginning with a vowel has an initial glottal stop, which is represented by *alef.* Thus the appearance of *alef* at the beginning of a word means in fact that it begins with one of the vowels. For dictionary purposes, all words beginning with *alef* are in the first group, regardless of the vowel.

5. Group II (Six Letters)

Joined to   Joined to   Joined to   Separate form   Basic shape
preceding preceding following
letter only and following letter only
          letters

All letters in this group carry distinguishing dots.

Pronunciation	Transcription	Joined forms	Name	Separate form
	b	ﺐ...ﺒ...ﺑ	be	ب (1)
	p	ﭗ...ﭙ...ﭘ	pe	پ (2)
as in English	t	ﺖ...ﺘ...ﺗ	te	ت (3)
	s	ﺚ...ﺜ...ﺛ	se	ث (4)
	n	ﻦ...ﻨ...ﻧ	nun	ن (5)
	y	ﻰ...ﻴ...ﻳ	ye	ي (6)

The *final* and *separate* forms of *nun* differ from the standard.

ﻦ ن

The *separate* and *final* forms of *ye* differ from the standard, and are generally written without the two dots.

ﯼ ﯽ

Letters preceding the final forms of *nun* and *ye* must be raised above the line in order to join at the correct point.

بی = *b–y*;　　　بن = *b–n.*

6. The Vowels

(i) a: slightly broader than the English vowel 'a' in 'cat'. This is represented by a short stroke . . . ˉ (*fat-he* or *zabar*) written over the preceding letter. Thus a word beginning with the sound *a* . . . would in writing begin ... اَ ; *b–a* = بَ , etc.

(ii) ɑ: about halfway between 'a' in 'father' and 'a' in 'wash'. This is represented by the secondary use of *alef*. Thus ا... would indicate the sound of . . . *a*. A word beginning with the sound *a* . . . would require to be written ... اا ; this is not considered very elegant, and so

the second *alef* is replaced by a long stroke written over the first, ... آ

(*madde*, not to be confused with the *fat-he* above). *b–a* = ... با , etc.

7. The Vowels (*cont.*)

(iii) e: approximately 'e' as in 'net'. This is represented by a short stroke written below the preceding letter ... ـِ (*kasre* or *ʒir*). Thus a word beginning with the sound *e* . . . would in writing begin ... اِ , *be* . . .

would be written ... بِ , etc.

(iv) i: approximately as 'ee' in 'sweet'. This is represented by the secondary use of *ye*, thus *i* . . . is written ... ایـ , *bi* . . . as ... بیـ , etc.

(v) ei: a diphthong similar to 'ai' in 'maid'. This is represented by *ye preceded* by the *fat-he*, thus *ei* . . . as ... اَیـ , *bei* . . . as ... بَیـ , etc.

Note. This combination only gives the diphthong when it is followed by a consonant or comes at the end of a word; followed by a vowel it remains a *y*..., e.g. بَیت verse—*beit*, پَی track—*pei*; but

بَیان explanation—*bayan*.

8. Group III (Four Letters)

| Joined to preceding letter only | Joined to preceding and following letters | Joined to following letter only | Separate form | Basic shape |

Letters preceding the last two forms above must be raised above the line, so as to join at the correct point.

In the printed form the preceding join is usually made as follows:

ح... ...ح...

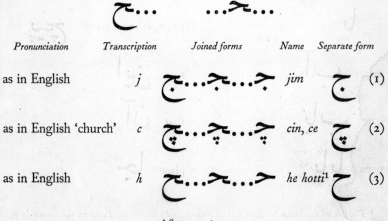

Pronunciation	Transcription	Joined forms	Name	Separate form
as in English	*j*	ج...ج...ج	*jim*	ج (1)
as in English 'church'	*c*	چ...چ...چ	*cin, ce*	چ (2)
as in English	*h*	ح...ح...ح	*he hotti*[1]	ح (3)

[1] See para. 89.

Pronunciation	Transcription	Joined forms	Name	Separate form
approximately as 'ch' in Scottish 'loch' or Welsh 'bach'[1]	x	خ...خ.ـخ	xa	خ (4)

The position of the dots in the various forms should be carefully observed.

9. Stress

The stress in Persian falls generally on the last syllable of the word. Suffixes, however, are not stressed unless they are regarded as forming an integral part of the word (see, for example, para. 28 *b*). Exceptions to the general rule are noted in paras. 49, 63.

VOCABULARY

with	با		without	بی
foot	پا		blue	آبی
until	تا		pocket	جیب
or	یا		twist, corner, screw	پیچ
water	آب		this	این
gate	باب		that	آن
papa	بابا		place	جا

---

[1] The use of the letter 'x' does not of course imply any resemblance to the sound of that letter in English.

here	اینجا	fever	تَب
there	آنجا	between	بَین
nose	بینی	desert	بِیابان
Haji, pilgrim	حاجی	soul, life	جان
verse	بَیت	bread	نان
track	پَی	body	تَن
see!	بِبین	explanation	بَیان

EXERCISES

A. Write as one word (reading from right to left) and translate:

2. چ+ی+پ   1. ب+ی+ج

4. ا+ج+ن+ی+ا   3. ب+ا+ب

6. ی+ج+ا+ح   5. ب+ی+ن+ی

8. ب+ا+ا   7. ب+َ+ی+ت

9. ن+ی+ا+ِ+ب+ِ+ب

B. Write as separate letters and translate:

١. آنجا ٢. این ٣. بابا

٤. آبی ٥. بَین ٦. تَب

٧. بِین ٨. بِیابان

C. Read and translate:

١. این جیب ٢. آن بِیابان ٣. با آب

٤. آب یا بِیابان ٥. بی جان ٦. بی نان

٧. تَن یا جان ٨. پا یا بینی

LESSON II

The Alphabet (*continued*). Case and Gender. Simple Sentences

10. Group IV (Two Letters)

Joined to preceding   Separate form   Basic shape
letter only

These letters are not joined to a following letter.

Pronunciation	Transcription	Joined form	Name	Separate form
as in English	*d*	ـد...	*dal*	د (1)
as in English	*z̧*	ـذ...	*z̧al*	ذ (2)

11. Group V (Three Letters)

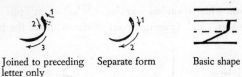

Joined to preceding   Separate form   Basic shape
letter only

These letters are not joined to a following letter.

Pronunciation	Transcription	Joined Form	Name	Separate form
trilled with the tip of the tongue	r	**ر**...	re	**ر** (1)
as in English	ẕ	**ز**...	ẕein	**ز** (2)
as 's' in 'pleasure'	ž	**ژ**...	že	**ژ** (3)

The letter 'r' must always be sounded, e.g. *barf* (snow, not *bāf*.

Compare also:

11a. Group VI (One Letter)

Joined to preceding   Separate form   Basic shape
letter only

This letter is not joined to a following letter.

Pronunciation	Transcription	Joined form	Name	Separate form
as English 'v' with tendency towards 'w'	v	**و**...	vav	**و** (1)

Note that Group IV letters join on the level of the main line of writing, whereas Groups V and VI join on the secondary line, requiring that preceding letters be raised.

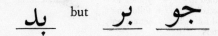

بد   but   بر   جو

12. The Vowels (*cont.*)

(vi) o: A somewhat rounded version of 'u' as in 'put'. This is represented by the sign . . . ُ (*ʒamme* or *piš*) written above the preceding letter.

Thus *o* . . . is written . . . اُ, *do* . . . as . . . دُ, *ʒo* . . . as

. . . زُ, etc.

(vii) u: 'oo' as in 'root'. This is represented by the secondary use of *vav*. Thus *u* . . . is written as . . . او, *ju* . . . as . . . جو,

xu . . . as . . . خو, etc.

(viii) ou: approximately as 'ow' in 'bowl'. This is represented by *vav* preceded by the vowel sign *fat-he*, thus *dou* . . . دَو,

rou . . . رَو

Note. This combination only gives the diphthong when it is followed by a consonant or comes at the end of a word; followed by a vowel it remains av . . ., e.g. نَو (new) = *nou*; نَوروز (new year,

lit. new day = *nouruʒ*), but جَواب (answer) = *javab*.

13. Group VII (Two Letters)

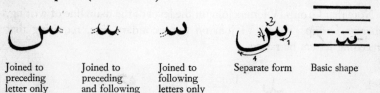

ـس	ـسـ	سـ	سِ	ـتـ
Joined to preceding letter only	Joined to preceding and following letters	Joined to following letters only	Separate form	Basic shape

Pronunciation	Transcription	Joined forms	Name	Separate form
as in English	s	سـ...ـسـ...ـس	sin	س (1)
as in English 'ship'	š	شـ...ـشـ...ـش	šin	ش (2)

14. Group VIII (Two Letters)

Joined to preceding letter only	Joined to preceding and following letters	Joined to following letter only	Separate form	Basic shape

Pronunciation	Transcription	Joined forms	Name	Separate form
as in English	s	صـ...ـصـ...ـص	sad	ص (1)
as in English	ẓ	ضـ...ـضـ...ـض	ẓad	ض (2)

15. Group IX (Two Letters)

Joined to preceding letter only	Joined to preceding and following letters	Joined to following letter only	Separate form	Basic shape

Pronunciation	Transcription	Joined forms	Name	Separate form
as in English	t	طـ...ـطـ...ـط	ta	ط (1)
as in English	ẓ	ظـ...ـظـ...ـظ	ẓa	ظ (2)

16. Case

There are no case inflections in Persian.

17. Gender

There is no distinction of gender, words which are naturally feminine being treated for grammatical purposes exactly as other nouns, e.g.

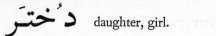 دُختَر   daughter, girl.

18. Sentence Structure

The normal sentence order is: Subject, Predicate, Verb.

حَسَن حاضِر اَست   Hasan is ready.

There is no definite article. The *a* of اَست, 'is' is usually elided

after a word ending in a vowel. This is sometimes also indicated in writing by the omission of the *alef*.

دُختَر زیباست   the girl is beautiful.

Alef may also be omitted after a consonant, and the ست written

joined to the word, e.g.

سیب شیرینَست   the apple is sweet.

Although separate pronouns exist (see para. 40), they need not be used as the subject of a verb.

حاضِر اَست   he is ready.

راضیست، راضی اَست   she is pleased.

The intonation pattern of a simple sentence of this kind is a rise followed by a fall (in the following examples, and throughout the book, the horizontal strokes indicate pitch, and the vertical strokes stress). The verb *ast* is not stressed unless it is contracted with a previous word ending in a vowel (see above).

hasan ‖ *hazer ast*		*in xabar* ‖ *sahihast*	
doxtar ‖ *zibast*		*baradar* ‖ *javan ast*	

EXERCISES

A. Read aloud and translate into English:

١. بانو زيبا ست

٢. باد تُنداَست

٣. اين خَبَر صَحيح اَست

٤. نَخَير، صَحيح نيست

٥. پِدَر خوب اَست

٦. آن سيب شيرين است

٧. نَخَير، اين سيب تُرش است

٨. دَر سَبز است

٩. شَب سَرد است

١٠. زَن حاضِراست

١١. بَرادَر جَوان است

١٢. اُستاد راضیست

B. Translate into Persian:

1. The girl is young. 2. The answer is not correct. 3. This apple is red. 4. That boy is Hasan. 5. Gold is yellow. 6. The door is open. 7. That apple is sour. 8. Hosein is not ready. 9. This lesson is difficult. 10. Reza is not pleased. 11. The boy is ready. 12. It is well (good).

VOCABULARY

answer	جَواب	lady	بانو
ready, present	حاضِر	wind	باد
(he, she, it) is	اَست	swift	تُند
daughter, girl	دُختَر	news	خَبَر
beautiful	زیبا	true, correct	صَحیح
apple	سیب	no	نَخیر، خیر
sweet	شیرین	is not	نیست
pleased, content	راضی	father	پِدَر

good	خوب	red	سُرخ
sour, bitter	تُرش	son, boy	پِسَر
door	دَر	gold	زَر
green	سَبز	yellow	زَرد
night	شَب	open	باز
cold	سَرد	Hosein	حُسَین
woman	زَن	lesson	دَرس
brother	بَرادَر	difficult	سَخت
young	جَوان	Reza	رِضا
master, teacher	اُستاد		

LESSON III

The Alphabet (*continued*). Number

19. Group X (Two Letters)

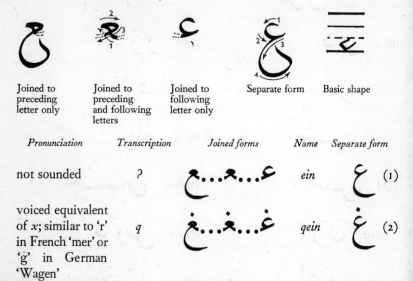

Joined to preceding letter only	Joined to preceding and following letters	Joined to following letter only	Separate form	Basic shape

Pronunciation	Transcription	Joined forms	Name	Separate form
not sounded	ʔ	ع...ع...ع	ein	ع (1)
voiced equivalent of *x*; similar to 'r' in French 'mer' or 'g' in German 'Wagen'	q	غ...غ...غ	qein	غ (2)

For further notes on the use of *ein* see para. 26.

20. Group XI (Two Letters)

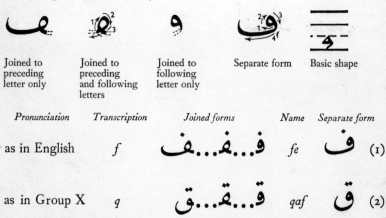

Joined to preceding letter only	Joined to preceding and following letters	Joined to following letter only	Separate form	Basic shape

Pronunciation	Transcription	Joined forms	Name	Separate form
as in English	f	ف...ف...ف	fe	ف (1)
as in Group X	q	ق...ق...ق	qaf	ق (2)

The separate and final forms of *qaf* differ from the standard:

21. Group XII (Two Letters)

| Joined to preceding letter only | Joined to preceding and following letters | Joined to following letter only | Separate form | Basic shape |

Pronunciation	*Transcription*	*Joined forms*	*Name*	*Separate form*	
as in English[1]	k	ک...ک...ک	*kaf*	ک	(1)
as in English[1] 'garden'	g	گ...گ...گ	*gaf*	گ	(2)

The two final forms of *kaf* are often written (and always printed) with a small sign ﮒ in the centre of the letter instead of the overhead stroke.

This sign may also be inserted in the *gaf*, but in this case the overhead strokes are retained. The second stroke of the *gaf* is sometimes replaced by three dots.

گ ﮎ

[1]Before the 'front' vowels (*a, e, i, ei*) and at the end of a word, these sounds become palatalized, the effect being somewhat as though a brief 'y' sound were inserted between the consonant and its following vowel, e.g.

کِتاب   book, *kᵛetab*.

22. Group XIII (One Letter)

| Joined to preceding letter only | Joined to preceding and following letters | Joined to following letter only | Separate form | Basic shape |

Note the level of the join preceding the final form.

Pronunciation	Transcription	Joined forms	Name	Separate form
as in English	*l*		*lam*	(1)

This sound must always be pronounced clearly, as in 'leaf', even when it falls at the end of a word. The English tendency to swallow it ('hall, bowl, real') must be avoided.

23. Group XIV (One Letter)

	alternative	alternative		

| Joined to preceding letter only | Joined to preceding and following letters | Joined to following letter only | Separate form | Basic shape |

Pronunciation	Transcription	Joined forms	Name	Separate form
as in English	*m*		*mim*	(1)

24. Group XV (One Letter)

	alternative			alternative	

| Joined to preceding letter only | Joined to preceding and following letters | Joined to following letter only | Separate form | Basic shape |

Pronunciation	Transcription	Joined forms	Name	Separate form
as in English	h	ﻪ...ﻤ...ﻬ...ﻫ	he havvez[1]	ﻩ (1)

This letter must always be sounded, e.g. شهر, town, *šahr*.

Secondary use of he. The final vowel of words that end in vowels must always be represented by a *letter*, even when elsewhere it would be represented by one of the *vowel signs*.

In the case of *a*, *i*, *u*, *ei*, *ou* no problem arises, since these are already represented by letters (ا ی و). Of the three remaining vowels, *a*, *e*, *o*, the sounds *a* and *o* are only found at the end of words in one or two isolated cases. The sound *e* in this position is represented by *he*.

خانه house, *xane*.

The final sound *a* is also represented by *he* in one word:

نَه (not, no!), *na*.

The final sound *o* is represented by *vav* in two words:

تُو (thou), *to*.

دُو (two), *do*.

It is important to note that, since *he* in this particular use is not a consonant but a symbol representing a final vowel, it may only be so used at the end of a word, and may not be joined to a following letter, e.g. to the first letter of a suffix. When a suffix has to be added to a word ending in

[1] See para. 89.

ه . . . , two alternatives are possible; either the *he* is dropped and the vowel

written in the usual way, or the suffix is written separately, e.g.

houses   خانه‌ها   or   خانها   (see para. 28 *b*).

The second alternative is preferred, as being less ambiguous. These rules
do not of course apply to *he* in its normal use as a consonant.

25. Writing Signs

A doubled letter is only written once, the doubling being indicated by
the sign . . . ّ (*tašdid* or *šadde*) written over the letter. This sign is
usually omitted in print and writing.

بَچّه   child, *bacce*.

Doubled consonants must always be pronounced doubled; cf. English
'boo*k*-*c*ase'.

When necessary to avoid ambiguity, a consonant that does not carry
a following vowel may be marked with the sign . . . ° (*sokun* or *jazm*).

دَسْت   hand, *dast*.

26. The Glottal Stop

Reference has already been made (para. 4) to the use of *alef* to represent
a theoretical glottal stop at the beginning of a word. In fact the sound is
really represented by the sign ء (*hamze*) written over the *alef*, but generally
omitted. This sound may also be found in the middle of a word and
(rarely) at the end; in such cases the *hamze* is generally written over a *ye*
without dots (occasionally also over *alef* or *vav*).

In certain cases (see para. 39) it may also be written over final *he*, when
this represents the vowel sound . . . *e*.

پائین   below, down, *paʔin*.

مَسئُول　　responsible, *mas?ul.*

مُؤمِن　　believer, *mo?men.*

مَأمور　　official, *ma?mur.*

The glottal stop, whether represented by *hamze* or by *ein* (see para. 19) is very weak in Persian. Between two vowels it is little more than a glide from one to the other. Between a consonant and a vowel it indicates a slight hesitation, between a vowel and a consonant a slight slurring of the vowel. When it follows a consonant at the end of a word, it has the effect of lengthening the preceding syllable without changing the quality of the vowel (this effect occurs in any word ending in two consonants).

رُبع　　quarter, *ro:b?.*

cf. سَخت　　difficult, *sa:xt.*

It may be noted that no Persian word can begin with two consonants. When foreign words of this type are incorporated into the language, a vowel is usually inserted, e.g.

اِستودیو　　studio, *estudyu.*

فِرانسه　　France, *feranse.*

27. The Silent *vav*

The letter *xa* at the beginning of a word is frequently followed by a silent *vav*. This *vav* has no phonetic or other value, and the word must be read as though it were not there.

خواهَر　　sister, *xahar;* but contrast: خون　　blood, *xun.*

خواب sleep, *xab*.   خوب good, *xub*.

خُود self, *xod*.

خویش self, *xiš*.

28. Number

(a) There is no article, either definite or indefinite.

Indefiniteness, in the sense of a single unspecified unit of a general class, is indicated by the suffix ی...

کِتاب book, the book.   کِتابی a book .

This suffix is not an integral part of the word, and is therefore not stressed. It may qualify more than one word, e.g.

کِتاب وَ قَلَمی a book and a pen.

یَک (usually pronounced *yek*) 'one' (see para. 88) is often used in the sense of 'a, an' either in place of or together with the indefinite suffix.

یَک کِتابی، یَک کِتاب a book.

(b) The normal plural ending is ها...)

کِتابها books, the books.

Rational beings, and certain other nouns, may alternatively take the

plural ending ان...

زَنان or زَنها   women.

This usage is commoner in the written than in the spoken language.

Both these suffixes are regarded as an integral part of the word, and
therefore take the final syllable stress (see para. 9).

A few words have special plural endings, e.g.

مَرد   man.

مَردان or مَردها   men (as opposed to 'women').

مَردُم   people.

With the exception of rational beings, plural nouns take a singular
verb. Adjectives (see also Lesson V), including demonstrative adjectives
(see para. 43), qualifying plural nouns of any class remain in the singular,
but when used as nouns or pronouns they take the plural endings, e.g.

بُزُرگان   great (men.)

آنان ،آنها   those (men, things, etc.).

But

این مَردُم   these people.

Note. (i) Words of Arabic origin may frequently be found with one
of the Arabic plural endings

...ین or ...ات

مَأمور official.   مَأمورين officials.

دَستور instruction.   دَستورات instructions.

(ii) Many words of Arabic origin form the Arabic 'broken' plural, which consists in an internal change in the form of the word (see para. 105).

كِتاب book.   كُتُب books.

سِرّ secret.   اَسرار secrets.

شَرط condition.   شَرایط conditions.

The Persian plural endings ان... or ها... may generally be used in place of these Arabic forms.

(c) In addition to the *Indefinite*, *Definite* and *Plural* uses of the noun, a *General* use is also possible, in which neither indefinite nor plural ending is used

این چیز کتابی است this thing is a book
                                     (Indef.).

کتاب آنجاست the book is there (Def.).

کتابها آنجاست the books are there
                                     (Plural Def.).

اینها کتاب است these are books (General).

این مَرد کارگِر است　　this man is a workman (General).

این مَردُم کارگِر اند　　these men are workmen (General).

29. Questions

No change of order is required to express a question. In speech the interrogative sense is indicated by the intonation; in the written style, when there is no interrogative word such as 'what?', 'why?', 'where?', etc., the question may be introduced by the particle آیا, e.g.

آیا حَسَن حاضِر است؟　　Is Hasan ready?

آیا دُختَر زیباست؟　　Is the girl beautiful?

Another similar particle, مَگَر, has a contradictory sense, expecting the answer 'no' to a question in the positive form, and 'yes' to a question in the negative form, e.g.

مَگَر دُختَر زیباست؟

Is the girl [really] beautiful? (Surely she isn't.)

مَگَر حَسَن حاضِر نیست؟

Isn't Hasan ready [yet]? (Surely he is . . . .)

The intonation pattern in questions follows a generally rising line:

(aya) hasan ‖ haẓer ast

(aya) doxtar ‖ ʐibast

The pattern is slightly different for the contradictory type of question.

$$\overline{} \ \underline{} \quad \underline{} \ \overset{\prime}{\underline{}} \ \Vert \ \overset{\prime}{} \ \underline{}$$

magar doxtar ‖ *ʒibast*

$$\overline{} \ \underline{} \quad \underline{} \ \underline{} \ \Vert \ \overset{\prime}{} \ \underline{} \ \underline{}$$

magar hasan ‖ *haʒer nist*

EXERCISES

A. Translate into English:

۱. این پِسَر وَ آن دُختَر خوب اَند

۲. اِصفَهان شَهری است

۳. این خانه بُزُرگ است

۴. قاشُق و چَنگال و کارد حاضِراست

۵. حُسَین پِسَراست و پَروین دُختَر

۶. آیا این شَرایِط سَخت نیست؟

۷. بَلی، این شَرایِط سَخت است

۸. راه دَراز است

۹. این وَطَن عَزیز است

۱۰. مَگَر اینجا آب نیست؟

۱۱. نَخیَر اینجا آب نیست

۱۲. این پِسَر بُلَند است و آن
دُختَر کوتاه

B. Translate into Persian:

1. These books are green. 2. Sleep is comfortable. 3. Persia is a country. 4. That child is small. 5. This knife is sharp. 6. That town is large. 7. The painter is ready. 8. The apple is red but the tree is green. 9. That book is wonderful and strange. 10. The mother is dear. 11. Is that house comfortable? 12. These instructions are easy.

VOCABULARY

and	وَ	fork	چَنگال
(they) are	آند	knife	کارد
town	شَهر	Parvin (female name)	پَروین
house	خانه	road (consonantal *he*)	راه
spoon	قاشُق	long (distance)	دَراز

condition	شَرط (شَرايِط pl.)		
fatherland	وَطَن	yes	بَلی
big, large	بُزُرگ	small	کوچِک
Isfahan	اِصفَهان	sharp	تیز
dear	عَزیز	painter	نَقّاش
long, tall	بُلَند	but	وَلی
short	کوتاه	tree	دَرَخت
comfortable	راحَت	wonderful	عَجیب
Iran, Persia	ایران	strange	غَریب
country	مَملِکَت	mother	مادَر
child	بَچّه	instruction	دَستور (دَستورات pl.)
sleep	خواب		
book	کِتاب	easy	آسان

LESSON IV

The Alphabet (*continued*) Writing Notes. Adjectives

30. The Complete Alphabet

¹ا.....	—	—	ا	ʾ	*alef*
ب......ب.....	ب	ب	ب	b	*be*
پ......پ.....	پ	پ	پ	p	*pe*
ت......ت.....	ت	ت	ت	t	*te*
ث......ش.....	ث	ث	ث	s	*se*
ج.....ج.....	ج	ج	ج	j	*jim*
چ.....چ.....	چ	چ	چ	c	*cin*
ح.....ح.....	ح	ح	ح	h	*he hotti*
خ.....خ.....	خ	خ	خ	x	*xa*
¹د....	—	—	د	d	*dal*
¹ذ....	—	—	ذ	z	*ẕal*
¹ر....	—	—	ر	r	*re*
¹ز....	—	—	ز	z	*ẕein*
¹ژ....	—	—	ژ	ž	* že*
س......س.....	س	س	س	s	*sin*

---

¹ These letters do not join a following letter.

ش...ش...ش	ش	š	*šin*
صـ...صـ...ص	ص	s	*sad*
ضـ...ضـ...ض	ض	z	*ẓad*
طـ...طـ...ط	ط	t	*ta*
ظـ...ظـ...ظ	ظ	z	*ẓa*
عـ...عـ...ع	ع	ʔ	*ein*
غـ...غـ...غ	غ	q	*qein*
فـ...فـ...ف	ف	f	*fe*
قـ...قـ...ق	ق	q	*qaf*
كـ..كـ..كـ..ك	ک ك	k	*kaf*
گـ...گـ...گ	گ	g	*gaf*
لـ...لـ...ل	ل	l	*lam*
مـ...مـ...م	م	m	*mim*
نـ...نـ...ن	ن	n	*nun*
و....	— —	و	v	*vav*
هـ...ﻬ...ه	ه	h	*he havvez*
یـ...یـ...ی	ی	y	*ye*

1

¹These letters do not join a following letter.

The above is the alphabetical or dictionary order. For the numerical order and values of the letters see para. 89.

31. Summary of Consonants and Vowels

Consonants

(a) Phonetic

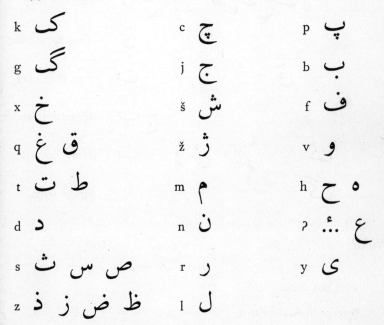

The duplication of sounds in the above list is due to the fact that certain letters (ث ح ص ض ط ظ ع ق) are found for the most part only in words of Arabic origin, in which language they have distinctive sounds. While in Persian the original spelling has been retained, the difficult Arabic sounds have been converted into sounds more acceptable to, and already existing in, Persian speech. The same applies to the letter ذ, though this is also found in a number of Persian words, and formerly stood for the sound '*th*' as in '*this*', no longer used in Persian.

c

(b) Writing

ا ح د ر س ص ط ع ک ل م و ه	No dots
ب ج	One dot under
ن خ ذ ز ض ظ غ ف	One dot over
ی	Two dots under
ت	Two dots over
پ چ	Three dots under
ث ژ ش گ	Three dots over
گ	Stroke over

Vowels

	End	Middle	Initial	
	does not occur	‌ـَ	اَ ...	a
	(except in نَه written	...	...	
	ه ... as ... e)			
	ـا	ـَا ...	آ ...	ɑ
	ـه	...	اِ ...	e
	ـَی	ـَیـ ...	اَیـ ...	ei
	ـِی	ـِیـ ...	اِیـ ...	i

	End	Middle	Initial	

only occurs in

تو and دو, written   ـُ   أ ...   o

و ... as ... u

ـ.َو   ...ـ.َو   أو ...   ou

ـ.ُو   ...ـ.ُو   أو ...   u

32. Summary of Writing Signs

used with following *ye* for *ei*, with *vav* for *ou* (may also be found with *alef* for *a*, and with final *he* for final *e*).	a	*fathe, zabar*	ـَ
(may be found with *ye* for *i*, and with final *he* for final *e*).	e	*kasre, zir*	ـِ
(may be found with *vav* for *u*).	o	*zamme, piš*	ـُ
used over *alef* for initial *a*.	a	*madde*	ٓ
used over *alef, vav, ye* (without dots), or without supporter, to represent glottal stop.	ʔ	*hamze*	ء
indicates that there is no vowel immediately following.	—	*sokun, jazm*	ـْ
sign of doubling.	—	*šadde, tašdid*	ـّ

Certain other writing signs will be mentioned in due course (see paras. 57, 108).

33. Punctuation

Older Persian books and manuscripts use little or no punctuation. Modern printed books use any or all of the following, but their employment is not yet standardized.

full stop   .

colon   :

semi-colon   ؛

comma   ،

dash   —

exclamation mark   !

question mark   ؟

quotation marks   ((   )) or (   )

Quotation marks are often omitted.

34. Handwriting Notes

(i) The following combinations of letters are used to avoid inelegant forms

(a) *lam* followed by *alef*.

This is used to avoid the form ‌ال. The following variants are found.

Joined form	Separate form
ﻼ...	لا

In some old grammar books this combined form is listed as a separate letter. It must always be used, the first variant being the commonest.

(b) *kaf* or *gaf* followed by *alef* or *lam*.

كا = ا... + ...ک

ـکا... = ا... + ...ک...

کل = ل... + ...ک

...کل = ...ل... + ...ک

ـکل... = ...ل... + ...ک...

کﻼ = ا... + ...ل... + ...ک

(c) Where several letters of Group II occur in succession it is usual to vary the height of alternate letters so as to avoid confusion.

تَنبَل or تَنبَل lazy.

(ii) It has already been pointed out that the *preceding* point of joining for a number of letter forms

...ع ...و ...ل ...ق ...ص ...س ...ی ...ن ...ر

falls on one of the secondary lines above the main line of writing whereas the *following* point of joining or the base of a final letter is invariably on the main line. To overcome this difficulty, the letter preceding one of these forms may be modified, or alternatively the whole of the initial part of the word may be raised above the line. These rules are not always observed in printed type and typewriter lettering, where modifications are introduced into the joined forms of certain letters.

(*a*) letters followed by Group V:

$$ـمر… = ـر… + …ـمـ…$$

$$…ـسر ، ـسر = ـر… + …ـسـ…or…س$$

$$…ـصر ، ـصر = ـر… + …ـصـ…or…ص$$

All other letters prefixed to Group V must be raised above the line.

(*b*) letters followed by final *nun*:

$$…ـمن = ـن… + …ـمـ…$$

$$…ـسن ، ـسن = ـن… + …ـسـ… ، …س$$

$$…ـصن ، ـصن = ـن… + …ـصـ… ، …ص$$

All other letters prefixed to final *nun* must be raised above the line.

(*c*) Letters preceding final *ye*:

$$…ـعی ، ـعی = ی… + …ـعـ… ، …ع$$

$$…ـکی ، ـکی = ی… + …ـکـ… ، …ک$$

$$…ـلی ، ـلی = ی… + …ـلـ… ، …ل$$

$$…ـفی ، ـفی = ی… + …ـفـ… ، …ف$$

$$…ـمی = ی… + …ـمـ$$

$$…ـبی = ی… + …ـبـ$$

$$…ـی = ی… + …ـمـ…$$

$$…ـسی ، ـسی = ی… + …ـسـ… ، …س$$

$$\text{صـ...، صـ...ـص...+...ى = صى ، صى...}$$

$$\text{...ـح...+...ى = حى}$$

$$\text{طـ...، ...ـطـ...+...ى = طى ، طى...}$$

It will have been noticed that the *preceding* letter forms that undergo the most marked modification are:

$$\text{...ـصـ...، صـ...، ...ـسـ...، ...ـس...، ...ـد...، د...}$$

In other cases it is rather the relative position of the letters that is important.

Great care must be taken to avoid duplication of the elements in these combined forms, for instance, ...ـص followed by ...ى must be written صى, and not صى, which would be read as though a letter of Group II with the dots missing were inserted in the middle.

(*d*) The following letter forms have the effect of raising the whole of the preceding part of the word above the line, without other modification:

final $\text{...ـس ، ...ـص ، ...ـق ، ...ـل ، ...ـو ، ...ـع}$

(*e*) Similar effects arise from the use of the handwritten forms of the letters in Groups III, XIV and XV, but these are not usually found in the printed form. Examples are:

Printed: $\text{...ـح ، ...ـنـ... ، ...ـنـ... ، كمـا ، نجـ...}$

Handwritten: حم صه ح ل

In printed texts the rules of calligraphy are not always carefully observed, but they are worth cultivating in handwriting, since they enter largely into the shape and style of the two handwritten scripts, *nastaʔliq* and *šekaste*, in which most manuscripts and letters (modern as well as mediaeval) are written.

35. Adjectives

Adjectives may be intensified by a preceding adverb, as خَیلی or بِسیار, 'very', e.g. very big خَیلی بُزُرگ; very good بِسیار خوب

These words may also be used as adjectives in the sense of 'much', 'many'.

اَست, 'is', is used when a complement or attribute is expressed.

دَر سَبزاَست   the door is green.

این عِمارَت پُستخانه اَست   this building is the post-office.

هَست, 'there is, exists', is used when there is no complement.

اینجا مَغازه هَست   there are shops here.

EXERCISES

A. Translate into English:

١. این مَنزِل بِسیار کوچِک اَست وَلی زیباست

٢. این أطاق خَیلی کوچِک نیست

٣. این زَمین است وآن سَقف اَست

٤. زَمین پائین است وَ سَقف بالا

٥. این دیوار بُلَند است

٦. اینجا پَنجَره هَست وآنجا دَر

۷. آیا آنجا باغی هَست؟

۸. بَلی خَیلی نَزدیک است

۹. این باغ سَبز است

۱۰. این گُل سُرخ است وَلی آن گُلها زَرد است

۱۱. آب لازِم است وَلی اینجا خَراب است

۱۲. این خِیابان خَیلی پَهن است وَلی آن کوچه تَنگ است

۱۳. بَلی آقا خِیابان بِسیار زیباست

۱۴. این مَغازه بِسیار مُفید است

B. Translate into Persian:

1. Is the bazaar far? 2. No sir, it is not far, it is near. 3. This bazaar is very beautiful. 4. There is fruit here. 5. Is this fruit fresh? 6. Yes sir, it is very fresh. 7. Is not this meat very expensive? 8. No madam, it is very cheap. 9. Is there [a] bank here?[1] 10. Yes sir, there is; it is there. 11. Is the manager here (present)? 12. Here is [a] table and chair and paper and pen and ink. 13. Is this building the post office? 14. No sir, it is there, but it is not open.

VOCABULARY

house	مَنزِل	much, many, very	خَیلی
much, many, very	بِسیار	ground, floor	زَمین
room	اُطاق	below	پائین

[1] Square brackets [ ] indicate words found in English, but omitted in Persian; round brackets ( ) indicate words required in Persian, whether additional or as alternatives.

ceiling	سَقف	sir, Mr	آقا
above	بالا	near	نَزدیک
wall	دیوار	fruit	میوه
window	پَنجَره	fresh, new	تازه
there is	هَست	meat	گوشت
garden	باغ	expensive	گِران
flower, rose	گُل	madam, Mrs, lady	خانُم
necessary	لازِم	cheap	ارزان
bad (things)	خَراب	bank	بانک
street	خِیابان	manager	رَئیس
wide	پَهن	table	میز
side-street	کوچه	chair	صَندَلی
narrow	تَنگ	paper, letter	کاغِذ
shop	مَغازه	pen	قَلَم
useful	مُفید	ink	جَوهَر
bazaar	بازار	building	عِمارَت
far	دور	post-office	پُستخانه

LESSON V

The Ezafe. Comparison of Adjectives. Hiatus

36. The Ezafe

(a) A second qualifying word (noun or adjective) may be linked to any noun by the *ezafe* construction, which consists in the insertion of the particle ... (*e*) between the two words. The qualifying word always comes second. The *ezafe* is an enclitic, that is to say, it is in the nature of an *unstressed* suffix to the preceding word. The following are among the commoner uses of this construction. (For another use see para. 58.)

(i) Possessive

Noun: کِتابِ بَچّه   the child's book.

پِسَرِ رِضا   Reza's son.

حُسَینِ رِضا   Hosein [son] of Reza.

دیوارِ خانه   the wall of the house.

(ii) Descriptive

Adjective: مَنزِلِ بُزُرگ   the big house.

دَرِ سَبز   the green door.

پِسَرِ جَوان   the young boy.

Noun: حُسَینِ نَقّاش   Hosein the painter.

راهِ اِصفَهان   the road to Isfahan.

پیرِ مَرد   old man (lit. 'man veteran').

پیرِ زَن   old woman (lit. 'woman veteran').

خانُمِ فَرهاد   Mrs Farhad.

(iii) Partitive

Noun: اَکثَریَّتِ زَنان   the majority of the women.

تمَامِ مَردُم   all of the people.

Similar to this is the Superlative construction (see para. 38*b*).

(*b*) The *ezafe* is used purely as a linking particle, and cannot appear except between a noun or nominal expression and an *immediately following* qualifying word or expression. However, several nouns and/or adjectives may be linked together:

دُختَرِ بُزُرگِ اَحمَد   Ahmad's eldest (lit. big) daughter.

پِسَرِ جَوانِ پیرزَن   the young son of the old woman.

رئیسِ کُلِّ بانکِ مِلّیِ ایران   the general manager of the National Bank of Iran.

Furthermore, any item in the chain may consist of more than one word (in which case the *ezafe* comes only between the two groups):

پِسَرِ آن مَرد   the son of *that man*.

پِدَر و مادَرِ آن پِسَر   *the father and mother* of *that boy*.

دُختَرِ جَوان و زیبا   the *young and beautiful* girl.

The last phrase could also be written

دُختَرِ جَوانِ زیبا   the young, beautiful girl

without significant change of meaning.

Where several words or expressions are to be linked in this way, *descriptives* take precedence over *possessives* and *partitives*:

اَکثَرِیَت ِ بُزُرگِ زَنانِ جَوانِ تِهران

the great majority of the young women of Tehran.

(c) The plural suffix is added to the noun in the usual way, but not to the qualifying adjective, which does not undergo any change (see para. 28)

زَنانِ زیبا   the beautiful women.

کُتُبِ مُفید   useful books.

Other suffixes, which do not form an integral part of the word, are added at the end of the complete group. Thus the 'indefinite' *ye* is used as follows in this construction:

مَنزلِ بُزُرگی   a big house.

دَرِ سَبزی   a green door.

پِسَرِ جَوانی   a young boy.

In an alternative construction the *ye* may be suffixed to the principal noun, in which case the qualifying word follows *without eẓafe*.

مَنزلی بُزُرگ   a big house.

دَری سَبز   a green door.

پِسَری جَوان   a young boy.

This construction may also be applied to partitives:

جَوالِ سَنگینی سیبِ دُرُشت   a heavy sack of large apples.

With this type of construction the verb in a sentence may often be inserted between the noun and the adjective:

حَسَن پِسَریست جَوان   Hasan is a young boy.

(d) A principal noun already referred to may, instead of being repeated, be replaced by the word مال ('property'), or از آن (lit. 'from (preposition, see para. 59) that') linked to the qualifying noun by *ezafe* in the usual way.

آن کِتاب مالِ حَسَن اَست   that book is Hasan's (lit. 'the property of Hasan').

این مَنزِلِ از آنِ رِضاست   this house is Reza's (lit. 'from that of Reza').

37. Other Qualifying Words

In a certain number of cases the qualifying word precedes the principal noun, in which case no *ezafe* particle is used. Among these are:

(a) the demonstrative adjectives این and آن, and compounds derived from these (see para. 43).

(b) Adjectives of number and quantity (including numerals) followed by the noun in the *singular* (see paras. 45, 88).

(c) Superlative adjectives, and adjectives of similar formation (see para. 38).

(d) Certain common adjectives, e.g.

خوب مَرد   good man.

خوب مَردی   a good man.

خوُش پِسَر   good boy.

The ordinary *ezafe* construction is also commonly used.

(*e*) Certain types of compound noun (see also para. 98). These are usually written as one word.

خوابگاه 'sleep-place', i.e. 'bedroom'.

روزنامه 'day-letter', i.e. 'newspaper'.

کارخانه 'work-house', i.e. 'factory'.

These forms are particularly common with words like

گاه (place),   نامه (letter),   خانه (house), etc.

cf. also

ایران زَمین   the land of Iran.

مَغرِب زَمین   the land of the west (i.e. Europe).

38. Comparison of Adjectives

(*a*) The Comparative is formed by the addition of the suffix ...تَر

کوچِکتَر 'smaller'.   بُزُرگتَر 'bigger'.

آسانتَر 'easier'.

The equivalent of the English 'than' is the preposition اَز (see para. 59):

پِسَر اَز دُختَر بُزُرگتَر اَست   the boy is bigger than the girl.

این دَرس اَز آن آسانتَراَست   this lesson is easier than that one.

The order of words in this type of sentence should be noted. This is the normal construction when two nouns are compared. When the comparison is between two actions, a different construction must be used (see para. 84*a*(*c*) (v), also para. 81).

(b) The Superlative is formed by adding the suffix تَرین...
to the positive form, e.g.

بُزُرگتَرین biggest.   کوچِکتَرین smallest.

آسانتَرین easiest.

Certain words form their comparative and superlative degrees from different roots, notably

خوب good.   بِهتَر better.   بِهتَرین best.

The Superlative may be used in two ways, differing very little from each other in meaning. In the first the superlative form is used as an adjective preceding the principal noun without *ezafe* (see para. 37(c)); in the second it is used as a noun linked to the following noun (put in the plural) in a more or less partitive sense (see para. 36(iii)).

بُزُرگتَرینْ مَنزِل the biggest house.

بُزُرگتَرینِ منازِلِ[1] این شَهر the biggest of the houses of this town.

The Superlative idea may also be expressed by using the comparative construction with هَمه 'all'.

این مَنزِل از هَمه بُزُرگتَر اَست this house is the biggest.

Note the following construction:

یَک اُطاق بیشتَر there is not more than one room
نیست (lit. 'one room, there is not more')

منازِل[1] 'broken' plural of مَنزِل

Similarly,

صَنْدَلی چیزی دیگر
نیست

> there is nothing but a chair (lit.
> 'a chair, there is not another thing').

39. Hiatus

Persian orthography does not permit of two vowels coming together
without a separating or buffer consonant. Thus when a suffix beginning
with a vowel has to be added to a word ending in a vowel, or a prefix
ending in a vowel has to be placed before a word beginning with a vowel,
it is necessary to insert either *hamze* (the glottal stop) or *ye* (in certain
cases other letters are also used). This spelling is in general reflected in
pronunciation, although, as has been pointed out, the glottal stop in
Persian is a very weak one, and often represents no more than a glide
from one vowel to another.

A. Suffixes

(i) Suffixes beginning with *a* or *a*, e.g. the *plural suffix* ان...., and
also the *pronominal suffixes* (para. 41) and certain *verbal* (para. 53) and
adjectival suffixes (para. 99).

(*a*) After words ending in ا.... or و.... the buffer letter is ی
(*ye*) for all suffixes, with the exception noted below.

آقایان gentlemen (from آقا sir, gentleman).

سُخَنگویان spokesmen (from سُخَنگو spokesman).

In certain cases the final و.... is resolved into و.... (*ov*), e.g.

bazovan بازوان arms (from بازو arm).

banovan بانوان ladies (from بانو lady).

(*b*) After words ending in ...ی the buffer letter is *ye* for all suffixes as in (*a*), but although sounded it is not written, the original *ye* of the word doing duty for both.

širaẓiyan شیرازیان Shirazis (from شیرازی Shirazi).

(*c*) After words ending in ...ه the buffer letter for the *plural suffix* ...ان... is ...گ... (gɑf), which replaces the *he* (this letter is a survival of an older Persian form, originally found in the singular as well).

بَچِگان children (from بَچّه child).

The *pronominal suffixes* will be dealt with in para. 41. The case of the *verbal suffixes* does not arise with words ending in ...ه. The *adjectival suffixes* are dealt with in para. 99.

(ii) Suffixes beginning with *i*, e.g. the *indefinite suffix*, and also certain *verbal* (para. 53) and *nominal* and *adjectival suffixes* (para. 99).

(*a*) After words ending in ...ا or ...و the buffer letter is ...ٔ (*hamẓe*), written over an undotted *ye*, for all types of suffix.

آقائی a gentleman.

بانوئی a lady.

(*b*) After words ending in ...ی the *indefinite suffix* is generally neither written nor pronounced.

صَندَلی the chair, a chair.

Occasionally a *hamze* ‥ؚ may be found written over the final *ye* of the word.

صندلیء

In verse, if the two syllables are required to be pronounced separately for the purposes of the metre, both *ye*'s may be written.

صَندَلیی

The other cases (*verbal, nominal* and *adjectival suffixes*) very rarely occur.

(*c*) After Persian words ending in ﻪ‥ؚ the *indefinite suffix* may be represented either by a *hamze* written over the *he*, the *ye* of the suffix being omitted, or by writing the suffix as though it were a separate word, that is, with an initial *alef*.

خانهٔ or خانهای a house.

The *nominal* and *adjectival suffixes* are dealt with in para. 99. The case of the *verbal suffixes* does not arise.

(iii) The Ezafe.

(*a*) After words ending in ا‥ؚ or و‥ؚ the buffer letter is ‥یؚ

پایِ مَرد the foot of the man.

بویِ گُل the smell of the rose.

(*b*) After words ending in ‥یؚ no buffer letter is required, though a *y* is sounded.

(*sandaliye* ...) <div dir="rtl">صَندَلیِ حَسَن</div> Hasan's chair.

(c) After words ending in **ه...** a *hamze* is written over the **ه...**, though a *y* is sounded.

(*xaneye . . .*)   خانهٔ پیرِزَن   the old woman's house.

Care must be taken not to confuse this group with Group (ii) above.

(iv) The two diphthongs **و...** and **ی...**, when followed by a suffix beginning with a vowel, are generally resolved into their component parts of short vowel *a* and consonant *v* or *y*. Thus *ou* becomes *av*, and *ei* becomes *ay*.

peiravan   پـَیـرَوان   followers (from پـَیـرَو follower).

paye . . .   پـَی آن مرد   (on) the track of that man (from پـَی track).

In the first case the *a* is often sounded *o* by assimilation, even though it is always written **...**: *peirovan*.

B. Prefixes

The only prefixes involved are: (*a*) the *ezafe*, (*b*) the *preposition* **بـِه** (see para. 59), (*c*) three *verbal prefixes* (see para. 53).

The buffer letter following the *ezafe* is the *hamze*, and no change in writing is therefore required, as this is already represented by the initial *alef* of the following word. This glottal stop should, however, be sounded fairly clearly.

خیابانهایِ این شَهر   the streets of this city.

39a. Intonation Patterns

Para. 36:

an ketab ‖ male hasan ast

in manzel ‖ az ane rezast

hasan ‖ pesarist javan

Para. 38:

```
      _   _   _            _
pesar az doxtar ‖ bozorgtar ast

      _   _   _          _   _
  in dars az ɑn ‖ ɑsɑntar ast

   _    _   _          _        _
in manzel ‖ az hame bozorgtar ast

   _   _        _   _
yak otɑq ‖ bištar nist

   _    _   _        _     _    _
sandali ‖ cizi digar nist
```

EXERCISES

A. Translate into English:

١. آیا دَفتَرِ آقایِ مُحَمَّدی اینجاست؟

٢. بَلی آقا خَیلی نَزدیكِ است

٣. این روزنامه مالِ پَرویز نیست

٤. روزنامه‌هایِ شَهرِ تهران خَیلی است

٥. بُزرگتَرین شهرِ ایران تِهران است ولی از
   آن زیباتَر اصفهان است

٦. آیا گوشتِ تازه هست؟

٧. بَلی خانُم ولی این گوشت از آن بِهتَر است

٨. هَمهٔ مَردُم راضی اند

٩. خوُشوَقت‌تَرین روزِ سالِ ایرانی عیدِ
   نَوروز است

۱۰. کوچکترین عِمارتِ اینِ خیابان مَغازهٔ کَفّاش است

۱۱. اینِ کارخانه بُزُرگترینِ کارخانه‌هایِ ایران است

۱۲. اَکثَریَتِ مَردُمِ کارگر یا دِهقان اند

B. Translate into Persian:

1. All the children are present. 2. The hair of the head of that girl is yellow, but this boy's is black. 3. This child's hands are dirty. 4. Ali's hands are cleaner than Faridun's. 5. Hasan and Hosein are Parvin's brothers. 6. Parvin is the daughter of the manager of the factory. 7. Is Reza smaller than Hosein? 8. No, he is bigger. 9. This deed (work) is the fault of that boy. 10. Hushang's sister is a pretty girl. 11. Is this building Hosein's house? 12. No, it is Hushang's.

VOCABULARY

office	دَفتَر	festival	عِید
newspaper	روزنامه	shoemaker	کَفّاش
Parviz	پَرویز	workman	کارگِر
Tehran	تِهران	factory	کارخانه
all, every	هَمه	majority	اَکثَریَت
happy	خوشوَقت	peasant	دِهقان
year	سال	all, whole	تَمام
Iranian, Persian	ایرانی	hair	مو

head	سَر	Faridun	فَریدون
black	سِیاه	fault	تَقصیر –
dirty	کَثیف	Hushang	هوشَنگ
Ali	عَلی	pretty	خوشگِل
clean	پاک		

LESSON VI

Pronouns and Pronominal Adjectives

40. The Personal Pronouns

The Personal Pronouns occur in two forms, as separate words and as suffixes.

(i) Separate

	Singular		Plural	
1.	مَن	I	ما	we
2.	تو	you	شُما	you
3.	او	he, she, it	ایشان	they

'It' and 'they', when referring to inanimate objects, are more often rendered by آن 'that' and آنها 'those' (see para. 43).

تو (the second person singular) is used only in addressing intimate friends, children, servants, and so on; in other cases شُما (the second person plural) is used in a singular as well as a plural sense (cf. 'vous' in French). Similarly, though less consistently, the third person plural may be used for the third person singular.

It will be recalled that تو is pronounced *to* (para. 24).

The separate pronouns may be used:

(a) as the subject of a sentence (see also para. 87).

او تَنبَل است   he is lazy.

This use is not essential, and in fact arises only when emphasis is needed.

(b) as the possessor (with *eẓafe*).

این مَنزِلِ تُو است   this is your house.

آن پِسَرِ مَن است   that is my son.

کِتابِ تازهٔ مَن   my new book.

این کتاب مالِ مَن است   this book is mine.

(c) as the object of a verb (see para. 54).

(d) after prepositions (see para. 60).

The pronouns may be used in conjunction with the demonstrative adjectives.

این کتابِ مَن   this book of mine (lit. this book of me).

آن پِسَرِ تو   that son of yours (lit. that son of you).

تو may be contracted in writing with است = تُست (the

purely orthographic و being dropped).

(ii) Suffixes

	Singular		Plural	
1.	...َم	my, me	...َمان	our, us

2. ...ـَت ْ   your, you   ـَتان ْ   your, you

3. ...ـَش ْ   his, him   ـَشان ْ   their, them
                her, her
                its, it

It is worth noting that the plural forms are the same as the singular with

the addition of ...ـان. The same rules apply to the use of the second

persons singular and plural as for the separate forms.

The pronominal suffixes may be used:

(*a*) as the possessor

كِتابَم   my book.

پِسَرَش   his son.

These suffixes, not being an integral part of the word, are not stressed;
if, therefore, it is desired to emphasize the possessive pronoun, the
separate form must be used.

كِتابِ مَن   *my* book.

(*b*) with prepositions (see para. 60).

(*c*) as the object of a verb (see para. 54).

These last two uses are confined mainly to colloquial speech (or writing
in colloquial style) and to poetry.

When a pronoun (separate or suffix) qualifies a series of words linked
by conjunctions or *ezafe*, it is attached only to the end of the group, e.g.

پِدَر و مادَر و خواهَرِ مَن   my father and mother
and sister.

مَنزِل و باغَشان   their house and garden.

A pronominal suffix can never be inserted between two words linked
by *ezafe*:

پِسَرِ بُزُرگَم   my elder (lit. big) son.

The pronominal suffixes may be used in the following construction, which is designed to give prominence to the logical subject of a sentence when it is not actually the grammatical subject.

این کتِاب | رَنگَش سُرخ است

this book's colour is red, this book is coloured red
(lit. 'this book, its colour is red').

تُو | مَنزِلَت این اَست؟

is this your house? (lit. 'you, is this your house?').

In this type of construction, which has many variations in Persian, the complete sentence is formed from (i) the *subject* and (ii) the *predicate*, itself a complete sentence whose only link with the main subject is a pronoun, not necessarily the grammatical subject of the verb.

41. Hiatus

After words ending in a vowel, the suffixes conform to the rules already given in para. 39 A (i). The only case that requires special note is that of words ending in ﻪ.... After this ending the suffixes are generally written as though they were separate words, i.e. beginning with an *alef.*

بَچّه اَم

my child.

خانه اَش

his house.

42. The Reflexive Pronouns

For further emphasis the word خُود 'self' may be used with either the separate or suffix forms of the pronouns.

خُودَم، خُودِ مَن

myself.

خُودَش، خُودِ او

himself.

این منزل مال ِ خودَم آست   this house is my own.

خودَش حاضِر آست   he himself is present.

In the same way خود may be used with a qualifying noun, either following or preceding:

خود ِ رَئیس   the manager himself.

خود ِ هوشَنگ، هوشنگ ِ خود   Hushang himself.

خود ِ پِدَرَم، پِدَرَم ِ خود   my father himself.

There is no plural form of خود:

خودَشان themselves   خود ِ بَرادَران the brothers themselves.

For the use of خود (and also خویش) without suffixes see para. 54.

43. The Demonstratives

این   this.

آن   that.

When used as adjectives, the demonstratives remain unchanged in the plural. Used as pronouns, they take the normal plural endings:

آنها، آنان

They are frequently found compounded with other words,

e.g. اینجا here, آنجا there (جا place); هَمان, هَمین the same

(هَم even); چُنین، چُنان such (چون like).

آن and این are commonly used in the sense of 'the former' and 'the latter'.

$$كِتاب وقَلَمی اينجاست؛ اين سُرخ است وآن سَبز$$

a book and pen are here; the latter is red and the former green.

44. Interrogatives

The interrogative words may be used as either pronouns, conjunctions or adjectives. As pronouns or conjunctions, they are generally placed as near as possible to the verb, as adjectives they immediately precede the word qualified.

كی، كه؟ who?

چه؟ what? e.g. چه كتاب؟ چه كتابی، what book?

كُدام؟ which? چه چیز؟ what (thing)?

چه is often found in compounds such as the following:

چِگونه، چه گونه؛ چِطَور، چه طَور what kind of? how?

With آست, كی and چه contract to چیست، كیست

The following are common interrogative conjunctions:

چون how?   چِرا why?

چَند how much?   كَی when?

كُجا where?

این مرد کیست؟   who is this man?

این کِتاب چیست؟   what is this book?

این چه کتابی است؟   what book is this?

کُدام پِسَر حَسَن است؟   which boy is Hasan?

آحوالِ شُما چِطور است؟   how are you? (lit. how are your conditions?).

دَستهایَت چِرا کَثیف است؟   why are your hands dirty?

ساعتِ دَرسِتان کَی است؟   when is (the hour of) your lesson?

دوستَت کُجاست؟   where is your friend?

Note that the interrogative word normally comes next to the verb.

45. Pronouns and Adjectives of Quantity, etc.

Adjectives of quantity (and also numerals, see para. 88) generally precede (without *eẓafe*) the noun they qualify, which is put in the singular. This is also true of compound expressions such as

این قَدر، چه قَدر، هَمه جور، etc. (see below).

(i) هَر 'each, every, any' is generally used as an adjective.

هَر کَس   everyone.

هَر سال   each year.

Compounded with certain words, هَر is equivalent to the English suffix '-ever'.

هَرچه   whatever.

هَرجا، هَرکُجا   wherever.

هَرجا هَست لازِم اَست   wherever it is, it is necessary.

Prefixed to چه and an adjective in the comparative, it is equivalent to 'as. . . . as possible'.

هَرچه زودتَر   as soon as possible (lit. whatever sooner).

(ii) هَمه may be used either as a pronoun, 'the whole, all' or as adjective, 'each, every':

همۀ سال   all (of) the year.

هَمه سال   every year.

هَمه کَس   every one (person).

هَمه جا   everywhere.

هَمه جایِ ایران   everywhere in (lit. of) Iran.

(iii)

چَند	some.	چَند کِتاب	some books.
چَند،	how many?	چَند کتاب؟	how many books?
چه قَدر	how much?	چِقَدر چای؟	how much tea?
چَندان	so many		
چَندین	several.		

خَیلی مَنزِل	many houses.	خَیلی	many, much.
بِسیار بَچّه	many children.	بِسیار	many, much.
زِیاد گوشت	much meat.	زِیاد	many, much.

or

گوشت ِ زِیاد

آنقَدر نان	so much bread.	این قَدر، آن قَدر	so much.
کَمی آب	a little water.	(یَک) کَمی	a little.
قَدری آب	some water.	(یَک) قَدری	a quantity, some.
بیشتَرْ کتاب	more books.	بیشتَر	more, most.
بیشتَر ِ مَردُم	most of the people.		
اندَک وَقت	little time.	اندَک	little.
اندَکی	a little.		
یک جُرده نان	a little bread.	یک خُرده	a bit, a little.
		یَکی	one, someone.
هَمه جور مغازه	all kinds of shop.	هَمه جور	all kinds.

(iv) هیچ 'any' may be used either as a pronoun or as an adjective. In both cases the verb must be put in the negative, though the negative particle may be omitted in the interrogative form. As in the case of adjectives of quantity (para. iii above), a noun qualified by هیچ is always in the singular, and may also take the indefinite suffix ...ی (cf. چه above).

هیچ نان نیست	there is no bread.
آیا هیچ آب هست؟	is there any water?
آیا هیچ آب نیست؟ هیچ نیست	isn't there any water? There is none.
هیچکس اینجا نیست	no-one (lit. no person) is here.

(v) دیگَر 'other' has the following uses as adjective and noun:

پِسَرِ دیگَر، دیگَر پِسَر	the other boy.
پِسَرِ دیگَری، پِسَری دیگَر	another boy.
دیگَری	another (person, etc.).
کَسی دیگَر	another person, someone else.
یَکی دیگَر	another (person, etc.).

Note. The last use is not to be confused with یَکدیگَر 'one another'.

45a. Intonation Patterns

All these sentences follow the general pattern of a rising intonation for the introductory part, followed by a falling intonation (at any rate where a statement is concerned). In the case of questions, where there is no interrogative pronoun, the sentence ends on a rising intonation; but in questions that have an interrogative pronoun, the stress, which is accompanied by a high pitch, falls on the pronoun, and the rest of the sentence has a falling intonation.

Para. 40:

in ‖ manzele tost

an ‖ pesare manast

in ketab ‖ male manast

Para. 43:

ketab o qalami injast ‖ in sorx ast o an sabz

Para. 44:

in mard ‖ kist

in ‖ ce ketabist

kodam pesar ‖ hasan ast

dasthayat ‖ cera kasifast

saʔate darsatan ‖ kei ast

EXERCISES

A. Translate into English:

١. مَنزِلِتان کُجاست؟

٢. مَنزِلَم هَمینجاست

٣. وِلایَتِ تو کُجاست؟

D

٤. وِلايَتَم اِصفَهان است

٥. آن شَهر چِطَور است؟

٦. شَهرِ خيلى خوبى است

٧. آيا مَسجدهايِ آنجا خيلى كوچک نيست؟

٨. نَخَير آقا چَندين مسجدِ بُزُرگ هَست

٩. اين كاغِذ مال شُماست

١٠. چه خَبَر است؟

١١. خَبَرِ خوبى است

١٢. هيچ خَبَرى آز اين بِهتَر نيست

B. Translate into Persian:

1. Who is that strange person? 2. His name is not known. 3. Whose are these books? 4. These are Hasan's, but those are someone else's. 5. Is my father present himself? 6. Which boy is younger? 7. Hushang is much younger than Ali. 8. What book is this? 9. It is a history book (book of history). 10. Every winter there is much snow. 11. How many houses are there here? 12. It is not known, but there are many.

VOCABULARY

where?	كُجا	manner	طَور
just here	هَمينجا	how	چِطَور
home (city, province, country)	وِلايَت	mosque	مَسجِد
what?	چِه	several	چَندين

any	هیچ	someone else	کَسی دیگَر
person	شَخص	history	تاریخ
name	اِسم	winter	زَمِستان
known	مَعلوم	snow	بَرف

LESSON VII

The Verb: Simple Tenses. Verbal Sentences

46. The Verbal Stems

The conjugation of all Persian verbs is founded upon two stems, generally known as the *Present Stem* and the *Past Stem*. Once these are known for any given verb, that verb may be conjugated according to the one standard conjugation existing in Persian.

(i) The 'dictionary' form of the verb is the *Infinitive* (for its uses see paras. 70, 86). The Infinitive of all verbs ends in either -*dan* or -*tan*.

خَریدَن	to buy.
آوَردَن	to bring.
کُشتَن	to kill.
دانِستَن	to know.
ساختَن	to make.
دیدَن	to see.

(ii) The *Past Stem* is formed by cutting off the suffix -*an*. Thus all Past Stems end in either -*d* or -*t*.

خَرید...	buy ...
آوَرد...	bring ...
کُشت...	kill ...

دانِست... know ...

ساخت... make ...

دید... see ...

There are no exceptions to this rule.

(iii) The *Present Stem* is formed from the Past Stem in a variety of ways.

(1) Regular

(a) Past Stems ending in -*id* lose this syllable.

خَر... buy ...

(b) Past Stems ending in -*d*, in which the penultimate letter is *n*, *r*, *a*, or *u*, lose the letter -*d*.

آوَر... bring ...

(c) Past Stems ending in -*t*, in which the penultimate letter is *f* or *š*, lose the letter -*t*.

کُش... kill ...

(d) Past Stems ending in -*est*, -*eft*, -*oft*, and -*ad* lose this syllable.

دان... know ...

(2) Irregular

(e) A large number of common verbs, *including* many in the above categories, form their Present Stems irregularly (after dropping the d/t), either by a change in the final consonant, or by some greater change— even a different stem altogether.

ساز... make ...

بین... see ...

Apart from isolated instances, this is the only type of irregularity found in the Persian verb. The Present Stems of irregular verbs are given in most dictionaries (including the vocabularies at the end of this book), and should be learnt in conjunction with the Infinitive.

It will be appreciated that the Present Stem is in fact the basic element in the verb, and that the other forms have been derived etymologically from it, the 'irregularities' arising out of the assimilation of the final consonant of the Present Stem to the dental of the Infinitive ending.

48. Endings and Prefixes

(*a*) Personal Endings

The simple tenses of the verb are formed by combining the above two stems with the following personal endings:

	Singular	Plural
1.	م ...	ـیم ...
2.	ـی ...	ـید ...
3.	(Pres. Stem only) ـَد ...	ـَند ...

No ending is used for the 3rd Person Singular of tenses formed from the *Past Stem*.

These endings must not be confused with the Pronominal Suffixes (see para. 40(ii)).

(*b*) Verbal Prefixes

Three prefixes are used in the conjugation of the verb.

(a) می..., denoting continuity or repetition of action.

(b) ...بـه, denoting an element of doubt or futurity.

(c) ...نَه, denoting the negative.

All these prefixes may be written separately or joined to the verb. In the second case the *he* of به and نه must be dropped. Contrary to the general rule laid down in para. 9, these prefixes attract the main stress in the word, though there may be a secondary stress on the last syllable. When two occur together (in practice only ...نَمَی = نَه می), the first takes the stress.

49. Tenses formed from the Past Stem

(*a*) The *Simple Past Tense* is formed by the addition of the Personal Endings to the Past Stem.

خَریدَم I bought.	خَریدیم we bought.
خَریدی you bought.	خَریدید you bought.
خَرید he (she, it) bought.	خَریدَند they bought.

(b) The *Imperfect Tense* is formed by adding the prefix مـیـ...
(denoting continuous or repeated action) to the Past Tense.

مـیـخَـریدَم	I was buying.	مـیـخَـریدیم	we were buying.
مـیـخَـریدی	you were buying.	مـیـخَـریدید	you were buying.
مـیـخَـرید	he (she, it) was buying.	مـیـخَـریدَند	they were buying.

50. Tenses formed from the Present Stem

(a) The *Present Continuous Tense* is formed by adding the Personal Endings to the Present Stem, and also the prefix مـیـ....

مـیـخَـرَم	I am buying.	مـیـخَـریم	we are buying.
مـیـخَـری	you are buying.	مـیـخَـرید	you are buying.
مـیـخَـرَد	he (she, it) is buying.	مـیـخَـرَند	they are buying.

(b) *The Present Subjunctive Tense* is formed by adding the Personal Endings to the Present Stem, and also optionally the prefix بـه....

بِـخَـرَم	(that) I may buy.	بِـخَـریم	(that) we may buy.
بِـخَـری	... you may buy.	بِـخَـرید	... you may buy.
بِـخَـرَد	... he (she, it) may buy.	بِـخَـرَند	... they may buy.

(c) The *Imperative* or *Jussive* is the same as the *Present Subjunctive*, except for the 2nd Person Singular, which has no personal ending.

بِـخَـرَم   let me buy.

بِـخَـرَد   let him buy, etc.   but : بِـخَـر   buy! (sing.).

Note. When the *Present Stem* ends in ... *av*, this becomes ... *ou* in the Imperative 2nd Person Singular.

رَفـتَـن go: Present Stem. رَو... (*rav-*), Imperative Singular. بِرَو (*berou*—see para. 12).

In speech the Subjunctive and Jussive/Imperative are usually distinguished by the stress, which in the former tends to fall on the personal ending, and in the latter on the prefix.

51. The Negative

The negative conjugation of the verb is obtained by prefixing the particle *na . . .* to the appropriate tenses. The prefix *mi . . .* is retained, but the prefix *be . . .* must be dropped.

نَمیخَریدَم   I was not buying.

نَخَریدَم   I did not buy.

نَمیخَرَم   I am not buying.

نَخَرَم   . . . I may not buy.

نَخَر   do not buy!

In more formal style the negative prefix . . .مَ may be used with the 2nd Person Imperative (though not with any other tense).

آنرا مَخوُر!   do not eat that!

52. Summary of Simple Tenses

Inflection	Stem	Prefix	Tense
Personal endings	Past	—	Past.
		می	Imperfect.
	Present	می	Present.
		(بِه)	Present Subjunctive.
		(بِه)	Imperative and Jussive.

53. Hiatus

(i) Personal Endings

After Present Stems ending in a vowel, e.g. نَمودن show, Present Stem نَما; گُفتَن say, tell, Present Stem گو, a buffer letter must be inserted before the Personal Endings. Before the endings beginning with *a . . .* (Singular 1 and 3, Plural 3) this is always *ye*; before those beginning with *i . . .* (Singular 2, Plural 1 and 2) it is always *hamze* written over a *ye* without dots (see para. 39 A).

. . . *a-am* = . . . *ayam*   . . .ایَم   مینمایَم   I am showing.

. . . *u-ad* = . . . *uyad*   . . .ویَد   میگویَد   he is saying.

$\ldots a\text{-}im = \ldots a\text{?}im$	...ائیم	مینمائیم	we are showing.
$\ldots u\text{-}id = \ldots u\text{?}id$	...وئید	میگوئید	you are saying.

Stems ending in other vowels are virtually non-existent.

(ii) Verbal Prefixes

When the verb begins with a vowel, a buffer letter must be inserted, unless the prefix is written separately. When the verbal vowel is $i \ldots$, the normal practice is to leave the original initial *alef* to represent a glottal stop inserted between prefix and stem. In all other cases, the buffer letter inserted is *ye* (in the case of ...می the buffer *ye* is not written, the *ye* of the prefix doing duty for both).

be-avar ...-	*beyavar* ...	بیاوَر...	
na-avar ...-	*nayavar* ...	نیاوَر...	
mi-avar ...-	*miyavar* ...	میاوَر... or	می آوَر...

(from آوردن, bring; Present Stem آوَر)

be-ist ...-	*be?ist* ...	بایست... or	به ایست...
na-ist ...-	*na?ist* ...	نَایست... or	نَه ایست...
mi-ist ...-	*mi?ist* ...		می ایست...

(from ایستادن, stand; Present Stem ...ایست)

be-oft ...-	*beyoft* ...	بیُفت...	
na-oft ...-	*nayoft* ...	نَیُفت...	
mi-oft ...-	*miyoft* ...	میُفت... or	می اُفت...

(from اُفتادن, fall; Present Stem ...اُفت).

54. Verbal Sentences

The normal order of a verbal sentence is: Subject, Indirect Object, Direct Object, Verb.

The Direct Object of a verb is indicated by the use of the postposition را (formerly a noun), which is suffixed to the word or group of words constituting the Object. This is not, however, used unless the Object is definite.

كِتاب را (كِتابرا) خَريدَم   I bought the book.

كِتاب خواهَرِ اورا ميخوانَم   I am reading his sister's book.

اين كِتابرا بِدِه   Give [me] this book.

When the Object is not definite, two uses are possible—the word with the indefinite suffix ی..., and the word without either suffix or post-position. The second gives the word a general or generic sense.

كتابی ميخوانَد   he is reading a book (some particular book or other).

كتاب ميخواند   he is reading (a book or books, the emphasis being on the action).

كتابرا ميخواند   he is reading the book (already referred to).

را... is suffixed to the Separate forms of the Personal Pronouns, which undergo no change except in the case of the 1st and 2nd Persons Singular [see para. 40 (i) (c)].

$$\text{مَن I.} \qquad \text{مَرا me.}$$

$$\text{تو you.} \qquad \text{تُرا you (acc.).}$$

These changes apply whether the pronoun itself is the object, or whether it is simply the last of the group of words composing the object.

مَرا ديد   he saw me.

اِسمِ تُرا ميداند   he knows your name.

In colloquial and poetical styles the pronouns as direct objects are often represented by the pronominal suffixes attached directly to the verb:

ديدَمَش   I saw him.

Sometimes the pronoun may be attached to some other word, in which position it must not be confused with its possessive sense.

بِخاكَش سِپُردَند   they buried him (lit. they entrusted him to (see para. 59) the earth).

When a pronoun used in a possessive or other sense refers to the *subject* of the verb of the sentence or clause *in which it occurs*, the word

خوُد (self, see para. 42) should be used without pronominal suffix instead of the ordinary pronoun.

كِتاب خودرا خوانْد   he read his (own) book,

but   كِتاب اورا (كتابَش را) خوانْد   he read his (someone else's) book.

The rule governing the use of this reflexive pronoun should be carefully noted, as its misuse may lead to confusion. This rule, however, need not apply when the pronoun خود is qualified by one of the pronominal suffixes.

54a. Intonation Patterns

The most important feature of these patterns is the stress on the verbal prefixes, which also attract a high pitch.

ketabra xaridam

ketab(i) mixanad

ketabe xahare ura ‖ mixanam

EXERCISES

A. Translate into English:

خیابانهای تهران بِسیار مَغازه دارَد. این مَغازهها هَمه جور جِنس میفروشَد. زَنِ مَن لِباسِ نَو میخَرَد. پیراهَنِ سَفید ودامَنِ سَبزی میخَرَد. من کُلاهِ تازه میخواهَم. یَکی اینجا میبینم. مَغازهٔ مُجاوِرِ کِتابخانه ایست. کِتابفُروش مَرا میخوانَد. میگویَد بِیائید، خیَلی کتابِ تازه دارم. همه را میآوَرَد. تازه تَرینِ آنها را نَدارم. کُلاهِ تازه نَمیخرم، آنها را میخرم.

B. Translate into Persian:

I was reading my book. Reza knocked [at] the door. He brought his friend Hasan. We drank tea and [ate] sweets. Hasan told the news of the town. He saw an accident. A careless driver was driving a car. He struck another car. The police came. They said, It is the fault of the first driver. They seized him and took [him] away. The streets of Tehran are very dangerous. Many vehicles come and go (are coming and going).

VOCABULARY

Present Stems of irregular verbs are given in brackets.

to have[1]	داشتَن (دار)	to come	آمَدَن (آ)
sort, kind	جور	to knock, strike	زَدَن (زَن)
goods	جِنس	to bring	آوَردَن
to sell	فُروختَن (فُروش)	to eat, drink	خُوردَن
clothes	لِباس	sweets	شیرینی
to buy	خَریدَن	accident	حادثه
shirt, blouse	پیراهَن	driver	رانَنده، شوفِر
white	سَفید	careless	غافِل
skirt	دامَن	to drive	راندَن
hat	کُلاه	motor-car	اُتومُبیل
to wish, want, ask for	خواستَن (خواه)[2]	policeman	پاسبان
to see	دیدَن (بین)	first	اَوَّل
neighbouring	مُجاوِر	fault	تَقصیر
bookshop	کِتابخانه	to take, seize	گِرِفتَن (گیر)
bookseller	کِتابفُروش	to carry, take away	بُردَن (بَر)
to call, read	خواندَن	dangerous	خَطَرناک
to say, tell	گُفتَن (گو)	(motor-)vehicle	ماشین
		to go	رَفتَن (رَو)

---

[1] داشتَن does not take prefixes می and به (see para. 71).

[2] Silent *vav* (see para. 27).

LESSON VIII

Adverbs. Prepositions. Conjunctions

55. Nouns used as Adverbs

Most nouns of time and many of place may be used as adverbs without change, either alone or qualified.

روز   by day.

روزی   one day.

شَب، شَبها   at night.

روزِ تَعطیل   on the holiday.

صُبحِ زود   in the early morning.

سال گُذَشته   last year.

هَفتهٔ آیَنده   next week.

هِنگامِ غروبِ آفتاب   at sunset (at the time of the setting of the sun).

ساعَتِ ناهار   at lunch-time (at the hour of lunch).

وَقتِ مُسافَرَتِ ما   at the time of our journey.

مَوقِعِ حَرَکت   at the moment of departure.

The following may be used as nouns, though more frequently adverbially:

اِمروز   today.

اِمشَب   tonight.

دیروز   yesterday.

دیشَب   last night.

پَریروز   the day before yesterday.

پَریشَب   the night before last.

فَردا   tomorrow.

فَردا شَب   tomorrow night.

پَسفَردا   the day after tomorrow.

فَردایِ آن روز   the day following that day.

The following nouns are mainly used as adverbs (or prepositions, see para. 58):

بیرون، خارِج	outside.
داخِل، تو	inside.
پائین	below.
بالا	above.
جِلَو، پیش	in front.
پُشت، عَقَب	behind.

56. Adjectives used as Adverbs

Any suitable adjective may be used as an adverb without change.

زود	quick, quickly, soon.
خَیلی، بِسیار	much.
کَم	little.
دور	far.
خوب	good, well.
تَنها	only, alone.
سَخت کوشید	he tried hard.

Many adjectives of quantity are used in this way, sometimes with the addition of the indefinite suffix ی...

بیشتَر، اَغلَب	more, mostly.
چَندان	somewhat.
هیچ	not at all, never.
هیچ وَقت	never.
دیگَر	more, again; (with neg.) (no) more, (no) longer.
چَندی	for some time.

57. Other Adverbs

A certain number of other words are currently used only in an adverbial sense.

هَم   even; also; together (usually follows the noun).

پَس   then, next.

نیز   also.

بَس   enough.

هَمیشه   always.

هَرگِز   never.

آکنون   now, at present.

هَنوز (still, yet) is normally used with a negative verb.

هَنوز نَیامَد   he has not yet come.

پیش, when used of time, has the sense of 'ago'.

یَک هَفته پیش   one week ago.

A number of common adverbs are borrowed from Arabic:

فَقَط   only.

حَتَّی (pron. *hatta*)[1]   even (usually precedes the noun).

یَعنی   that is to say.

عَلَیحَدّه (pron. *alahadde*)[1]   separately.

حالا   now.

آلآن (*alʔan*)   just now, directly, presently.

اَلبَتّه   certainly.

---

[1] In a certain number of words of Arabic origin a final *a* is represented by a *ye* preceded by *fathe* (instead of the usual *alef*). Occasionally *ye* is so used in the middle of a word (in fact between two words run together): عَلَیحَدّه for عَلَی حَدّه (Arabic = 'on its limit').

Some of these still retain the Arabic Accusative ending . . . *an* (used in Arabic to form adverbs). This is written as a doubled *fathe* followed by *alef.* ً اً . . . .

أَصْلاً	originally, at all.	أَخيراً	lately.
فِعْلاً	actually.	سابِقاً	formerly.
تَقْريباً	nearly.	طَبْعاً	naturally.
أَقَلاً	at least.	كامِلاً	completely.

A variant on this spelling is found in words retaining the Arabic feminine ending in the same case, . . . *atan*. This is written as a *he* with two dots over it and the doubled *fathe*, but no *alef:* ةً . . .

حَقيقَةً	really, truly.
نِسبَةً	relatively.
عَجالَةً	for the time being.

A common error, found even in Persian books, is to spell these as though they belonged to the first group, with تاً . . . . A more serious error, but one also found occasionally in Persian books, is to use the spelling ةً . . . for certain adverbs ending in . . . *atan*, where this is not, in fact, the Arabic feminine, e.g.

(correct spelling) مُوَقَّتاً temporarily (from root وقت, see paras. 103, 106).

Sometimes this Arabic suffix is attached to a Persian or European word:

تِلِفوناً by telephone.

58. Prepositional Expressions

The great majority of the words used to render prepositions in Persian are nouns or adverbs, some of them obsolete in any other use but this, but most of them still current. As such, they are naturally linked to the word they govern by the *ezafe*.

رو	on (lit. face).	روی میز	on the table.
سَر	on (lit. head).	سَر کوه	on the mountain.

جا   instead of (lit.   جایِ مَن   instead of me.
place).

دَم   at, near (lit. mouth,   دَمِ دَر   at the door.
breath).

طَرَف، سو   towards (lit. side, direction).

...آن طَرَفِ   on that (the far) side of.

...این طَرَفِ   on this (the near) side of.

داخِل، تو   inside.

خارِج، بیرون   outside.

پُشت   behind (lit. back).   پُشتِ دَر   behind the door.

بالا   above.

پائین   below, at the foot of.

زیر   beneath.

پیش   near, in the presence (company) of, in front of.

جِلَو   in front of.

پَس، عَقَب   behind.

نَزد، نَزدیک   near.

بَین، میان   between, in the midst of.

The form بَرایِ, the usual word for 'for', is an archaic combination of *ba-* (= modern *be-*) and *ra* (see para. 54).

این کاغِذ بَرایِ عَلی است   this letter is for Ali.

59. Prepositions

The following (apart from a few rarities) are the only true prepositions in Persian. They are not followed by the *ezafe*.

از   from.   به   to, with (instrumental).

با   with, in company with.   بَر   on.

دَر in.   جُز except.

بی without.   مَگَر except.

تا as far as, until.   چون like.

The first four are used idiomatically after a large number of verbs.

از منزل خود رفت   he went from his house.

کتابرا از بچه گرفت   he took the book from the child.

با پسر خود آمد   he came with his son.

سیبی بمن داد   he gave (to) me an apple.

باصفهان رفت   he went to Isfahan.

بر صندلی نشست   he sat on the chair.

تا اصفهان رفت   he went as far as Isfahan.

دَر أطاق کسی نبود   there was no one in the room.

کاملًا بی پول است   he is completely without money.

جُز او کسی نبود   there was no one except him.

(a) از is frequently found as the second element in compound prepositions, in which the other element is an adverb.

قَبَل آز، پیش از before (time).

e.g. پیش ْ از ناهار before lunch.

but پیش ِ آن منزل in front of that house.

بعد از، پَس از after (time).

غَیر از other than, besides.

Apart from its use with comparative adjectives (see para. 38), از also has a partitive use, generally after a noun of quantity with the indefinite ی..., though the prepositional phrase may also stand by itself as the subject or object of a verb. In this use it may replace the *ezafe* construction where the first noun is required to be indefinite and the second definite.

بِسیاری از شَهرها   many of the cities.

چَندی از مردم   some of the people.

بَعضی از بچه‌ها   some of the children.

یَکی از ایشان   one of them.

هیچ یَکی از مَردُم   none of the people.

فِهرِستی از کِتابها   a list of the books.

از آن سیبها بِده   give [me some] of those apples.

از مردمِ شَهر حاضر بودند   [some] of the townspeople (people of the town) were present.

(b) بِه may be written either separately or joined to the following word (in which case the *he* is dropped).

به مَنزِلَم، بمَنزِلم   to my house.

When preceding a word beginning with an *alef* (i.e. with a vowel) it may be written either separately or joined, but in the second case the *alef* continues to be written, even though it is no longer the initial letter (see para. 39 B above).

بِایران or به ایران   to Iran.

به او or باو، بِآن or به آن، باین or به این..   to this . . ., to that . . ., to him.

Before این، آن and او a *d* is often inserted in place of the *alef*.

بِدین، بِدان، بِدو   to this, to that, to him.

بِه has a great many idiomatic uses, and is also frequently used in compounds with other prepositions (see para. 60).

اورا بِچوب زَدَند   they beat him with [a] stick.

بنَظَرِ من   in my opinion.

این را بِیِک تومان میدِهَم   I [will] give [i.e. sell] this for one *tuman*.

این منزل بِبُزُرگیِ آن نیست   this house is not as big as that [one].

(c) بَر is comparatively rarely used by itself in current Persian, but is commonly prefixed to prepositional expressions with similar meaning (see para. 60). It is also found in such compound prepositions as بَنابَر, مَبنی بَر 'according to' (lit. 'based upon, building upon').

بَنا بَر این   accordingly, therefore.

مَبنی بَر دستوراتِ رَئیس   according to the instructions of the

manager.

60. Compound Prepositions

These prepositions are frequently used with the prepositional expressions listed in para. 58, with such modifications of meaning as arise naturally.

بَررو، بَرسَر	on.
بِجا	instead of.
بِطَرَف	towards.
اَز بیرون	from outside.
دَر میان	in between.
تا پائین	as far as the foot of.
بِجِلَو	to the front of.

All prepositions and prepositional expressions may be used with the separate forms of the pronouns; in poetry and colloquial usage it is also common to use them with the pronominal suffixes.

اَز او   or   اَزَش   from him.

پُشتِ شُما   or   پُشتِتان   behind you.

پیش is often used to replace the verb 'to have', e.g.

کِتاب پیشِ مَن است   I have the book.

Where a preposition governs a series of nouns linked by 'and', it is not necessary to repeat it.

مَردُم در کوچه‌ها و خیابانها ومیدانها آند   The people are in the side-streets,

streets and squares.

61. Prepositional Adjectives and Adverbs

Prepositional groups, e.g. nouns governed by prepositions, may often be used to qualify nouns, using the ordinary *eẓafe* construction. Some of these instances are so common as to have attained the status of adjectives, and may take the comparative and superlative endings (see para. 100c).

مَنْزِلِ پُشْتِ آن عِمارَت	the house behind that building.
نَوکَرِ باوَفا	the loyal servant (lit. with loyalty).
دُشمَنِ بی وَفا	the treacherous enemy (lit. without loyalty).
بی وَفاتَرین دُشمَن	the most treacherous enemy.

Prepositions may be used sometimes with adverbs:

تاکُنون	till now.
باهَم	together.

62. Co-ordinating Conjunctions

The following conjunctions are among the commoner ones used to link independent sentences (for those used with subordinate clauses see Lessons x, xi, xii).

وَ ، (va) ، وُ (o)	and.
وَلی، وَلیکِن، لیکِن، آمّا	but.
یا، وَیا	or.
هَم ...هَم، چه...چه	both ... and.
یا...(وَ)یا، خواه...خواه	either ... or.
نَه...(وَ)نَه	neither ... nor.
بَلکه	or rather, perhaps.
مَگَر	surely ... ? (used with negative verb when expecting the answer 'yes', and vice versa—see para. 29).
مَگَر اینجا نیست؟	isn't he here? (i.e. surely he is).

In a series of closely linked words, وَ generally takes the enclitic
(i.e. *unstressed* suffix) form *o* :

پِدَرُو مادَرُو خواهَرُو بَرادَرِ مَن   my father and mother and

حاضِراند   brother and sister are here.

  (i.e. *pedaro madaro . . .*)

In less close links, and especially in linking sentences, the usual form
is وَ (*va*) (which sometimes carries a slight stress).

مادَرِ مَن اینجاست وَپِدَرِمَن آنجا   my mother is here and my
father there.

  (i.e. . . . . *injast va pedar-e man . . .*)

But it should be noted that there is no orthographical change to
indicate which is to be used, and in fact the choice lies with the individual
taste of the speaker or reader. Thus, in both the above examples, the
opposite forms could be used without altering the sense.

Various adverbs and adverbial expressions often take the place of
conjunctions.

هَم   also.

پَس   then.

آنوَقت   then (lit. at that time).

بَنابَراین   therefore, etc.

63. Word Order and Stress

Reference was made in paras. 18 and 54 to the word order of a simple
sentence. Where adverbial and other expressions are involved, the order is
as follows, though this may be altered where required for special emphasis.

Subject/Adverbial Expressions: (*a*) Time. (*b*) Place/Attribute or
Complement/Direct Object/Compound Element in Verb (see para. 72)/
Finite Verb.

It is, however, quite usual for the Adverbial Expression of Time to
be placed at the beginning of the sentence, especially when it links in
some way with the preceding statement. Similarly in colloquial style

(especially in narrative) an Adverbial Expression of Place may *follow* such verbs as 'go', 'come', 'look', etc.

صُبح ِ زود پِسر ِ نَجّار ِفت خانه   early in the morning the son of the carpenter went home.

As stated in para. 9, the guiding rule is that the main stress falls on the last integral syllable of the word. The main exceptions to this are: (a) verbal forms carrying one of the stressed verbal prefixes (para. 49), (b) particles and conjunctions with the general meanings of 'yes' and 'no' (بَلکه، لیکِن، وَلی، اَمّا، 'but' (آری، بَلی، نَخیَر), 'perhaps' (بَلکه، گویا، شایَد), in all of which the main stress tends to fall on the first syllable.

63a. Intonation Patterns

The 'step-by-step' rising intonation in the third and fourth examples should be noted.

Para 58:

in kɑqez ‖ barɑye alist

Para. 60:

ketab ‖ piše manast

mardom ‖ dar kuceha va xiyɑbanha va meidɑnha ʔand

Para. 62:

pedaro mɑdaro xɑharo barɑdare man ‖ hazerand

mɑdare man injɑst va ‖ pedare man ɑnjɑ

magar injɑ nist?

EXERCISES

A. Translate into English:

روزی مُلّا نَصرُ الدّین پیش ِ شیرینی فُروش رَفت، شیرینی خیَلی
میخواست اَمّا دیناری در جیبش نبود. پَس داخِل ِ دُکّان رفت شیرینی

میخورد. صاحب دُکّان پول میخواست مُلّا نَشَنید. صاحبِ دکان
عَصَبانی شُد مُلّا را چَند بار با چوب زَد. مُلّا هَمیشه شیرینی میخورد
وگُفت «چه شهرِ خوبیست وچه مَردُمِ مِهرَبانی دارد، غَریبانرا بِضَربِ
چوب میزَنَند ومیگویَند باز هَم شیرینی بِخور».

B. Translate into Persian:

Persia is a very old country. Civilized men lived there more than
seven thousand years ago. The most important centre of civilization was
Susa. Nearly three thousand years ago the Aryan tribes came to Persia
from Central Asia. They were the ancestors of the Persians of today.
They built the cities of Hamadan and Persepolis. During (In) this period
the prophet Zoroaster taught a new religion. The most famous king of
the Persians was Darius the Achaemenian. At the end (In the last parts)
of the sixth century B.C. he took the whole of Persia, Mesopotamia,
Syria, and Egypt, and sent his armies into India. After two hundred years
Alexander the Greek defeated the Persian armies, and the last king of the
Achaemenian dynasty died.

VOCABULARY

molla, priest	مُلّا	owner	صاحِب
Molla Nasroddin [1]	مُلّا نَصرُ الدین	money	پول
near, in the presence of, 'chez'	پیش	to hear	شَنیدَن (شنَو)
confectioner	شیرینی فُروش	angry	عَصَبانی
but	آمّا	to become	شُدَن (شَو)
dinar (small coin)	دینار	time	بار
in	دَر	wood, stick	چوب
to be	بودَن (باش)	to strike	زَدَن (زَن)
then	پَس	always	هَمیشه
inside	داخِل	to say	گُفتَن (گو)
shop	دُکّان	kind (adj.)	مِهرَبان

[1] For spelling see para. 108.

with به

blow ضَرب

again باز

old, ancient قَدِيم

civilized مُتَمَدّن

to live زِيستَن (زِى)

seven [see paras. 45 (iii), 88] هَفت

thousand هَزار

important مُهِمّ

centre مَرکَز

civilization تَمَدُّن

Susa شوش

three [see paras. 45 (iii), 88] سه

tribe (pl. ايلات) ايل

Aryan آريائى

Asia آسيا

central مَرکَزى

ancestor (pl. آجداد) جَدّ

to build ساختَن (ساز)

Hamadan هَمَدان

Persepolis تَختِ جَمشيد

period دَوره

Zoroaster زَردُشت

prophet پَيغَمبَر

religion دين

to teach آموختَن (آموز)

famous مَشهور

king پادشاه

Darius داريوش

Achaemenian هَخامَنِشى

last parts آواخِر

century قَرن

sixth (see para. 90) شِشُم

B.C. قَبل آز ميلاد

Mesopotamia عِراق

Syria سوريه

Egypt مِصر

army لَشگَر

India هِند، هِندوستان

to send فِرِستادَن (فِرِست)

two hundred [see paras. 45 (iii), 88)] دَويست

Alexander اِسکَندَر

Greek, Roman رومى

to defeat, break شِکَستَن (شِکَن)

last آخِرين

dynasty خاندان

to die مُردَن (مير)

LESSON IX

The Verb: Compound Tenses. Uses of Tenses. Compound Verbs

64. The Past Participle

The only participle used in the conjugation of the verb is the *Past Participle*. This is formed by adding ‌ه... to the *Past Stem*.

خَریده   bought.

آوَرده   brought.

کُشته   killed.

دانسته   known.

ساخته   made.

دیده   seen.

This participle is also used as an adjective (see para. 7●).

65. Auxiliaries

The following verbs, besides having their normal meanings, are also used as auxiliary verbs in the formation of compound tenses.

بودن   to be, present stem   باش

خواستن   to wish, present stem   خواه

شُدَن   to become, present stem   شَو

All these are conjugated in the normal way. There are however two additional verbs used for the present tense of 'to be'.

(a)   م...،آم   I am.   ‌یم...،ایم   we are.

ی...،ای   you are.   ‌ید،...اید   you are.

‌ست...،آست   he (she, it) is.   ‌نَد...،آند   they are.

This is the only form used as an auxiliary in the conjugation of other verbs, and is generally enclitic, i.e. unstressed. Otherwise, it has the simple meaning of 'to be' and requires a complement. It may be written separately or joined to the preceding word, and must not be confused with the personal endings of the verb (see para. 48).

(b)   هَسْتَم   I am.   هَسْتیم   we are.

      هَسْتی   you are.   هَسْتید   you are.

      هَسْت   he (she, it) is.   هَسْتَند   they are.

This has rather the meaning of 'to exist', 'there is', etc., and requires no complement, while the regular Present Tense (میباشَم, etc.) contains an element of doubt or futurity. Some interchange is also permissible for the sake of euphony or style.

The negative of both اَم, etc., and هَسْتَم, etc., are formed as follows:

نیستَم   I am not.   نیستیم   we are not.

نیستی   you are not.   نیستید   you are not.

نیست   he (she, it) is not.   نیستَند   they are not.

66. Compound Tenses

The Compound Tenses fall into three groups, the *Perfect*, the *Future*, and the *Passive*.

(i) The *Perfect* Tenses are formed by combining the *Past Participle* with the appropriate tenses of بودَن.

Perfect (Present tense of بودن):

خَریده اَم   I have bought.   خریده ایم   we have bought.

خَریده ای   you have bought.   خریده اید   you have bought.

خریده اَست   he (she, it) has bought.   خریده اَند   they have bought.

The prefix می is sometimes used with this tense, giving the sense of 'used to': میخریده اند they used to buy.

Pluperfect (Past tense of بودن):

خریده بودَم   I had bought.   خریده بودیم   we had bought.

خریده بودی   you had bought.   خریده بودید   you had bought.

خریده بود   he (she, it) had bought.   خریده بودَند   they had bought.

Perfect Subjunctive (Subjunctive of بودن):

خریده باشیم (that) we may have | خریده باشم (that) I may have
bought. | bought.

... خریده باشید you may have | ... خریده باشی you may have
bought. | bought.

... خریده باشند they may have | ... خریده باشد he (she, it) may
bought. | have bought.

Note that the Subjunctive of بودن never takes به.

(ii) The *Future* is formed by using the *Present Tense* of خواستن 'wish', *without* می, followed by the *Past Stem* (actually a shortened form of the *Infinitive*) of the verb

خواهم خرید   I will buy.   خواهیم خرید   we will buy.

خواهی خرید   you shall buy.   خواهید خرید   you shall buy.

خواهد خرید   he (she, it)   خواهند خرید   they will buy.
will buy.

Note that the Future sense may also be expressed by the Present Tense [see para. 68(c)].

(iii) The *Passive Voice* is formed by using the *Past Participle* together with the complete conjugation of شدن.

خریده شد   it was bought.

خریده میشد   it was being bought.

خریده میشود   it is (being) bought.

خریده شود   ... it may be bought.

خریده شو   be bought!

خریده شده است   it has been bought.

خریده شده بود   it had been bought.

خریده شده باشد   ... it may have been bought.

خریده خواهد شد   it will be bought.

67. Negative Compound Tenses

The negative is formed, as in the simple tenses, by prefixing the particle نَه to the complete verbal group.

نَخَریده اَم   I have not bought.

نَخَریده بودَم   I had not bought.

نَخَریده باشَم   ... I may not have bought.

نَخواهَم خرید   I will not buy.

N.B. The negative forms نیسَم, etc. (para. 65) are *not* used in the conjugation of the verb.

In the case of the *Passive* conjugation, however, the Past Participle itself is not regarded for this purpose as part of the verbal group, the negative particle being prefixed only to the various parts of شدن.

خریده نَشُد   it was not bought.

خریده نَمیشُد   it was not being bought.

خریده نَمیشَوَد   it is not being bought.

خریده نَشَوَد   ... it may not be bought.

خریده نَشَو   do not be bought!

خریده نَشُده اَست   it has not been bought.

خریده نَشُده بود   it had not been bought.

خریده نَشُده باشَد   ... it may not have been bought.

خریده نَخواهَد شُد   it will not be bought.

68. Uses of the Tenses

(a) *Past:* a single completed action in the past.

رَفت   he went.

اَلآن رَفت   he has just gone (Amer. he just went).

(b) *Imperfect:* continuous, indefinite or repeated action in the past.

میرَفت   he was going, he used to go.

In certain cases (see paras. 76, 85) it is used to express a past action that did not in fact take place.

(*c*) *Present:* generally used of action going on at the time of speaking,

میرَوَد he is going,

but also of habitual action

هَرروز میرَوَد he goes every day,

and of action in the future

فَردا بِشهر میرَوَم I am going to town tomorrow.

(*d*) *Present Subjunctive:* used for dependent verbs in the construction of various types of complex sentence (see Lessons x–xii).

N.B. The *Present Subjunctive* must not be used to render expressions like 'I might go', 'I should go', 'I would like to go', etc. These will be dealt with in para. 75.

(*e*) *Imperative* and *Jussive:* a simple command, permission or prohibition.

بِرَو ! go!   بِرَوَد ! let him go!   نَرَو ! don't go!

نَرَوَد don't let him go! (lit. 'let him not go!').

(*f*) *Perfect:* a single action in the past the effects of which are still continuing or are still felt.

رَفته آست he has gone (and is not back yet).

(*g*) *Pluperfect:* a past action related to another past but later action (mainly used in or in conjunction with Subordinate Clauses, see Lessons x–xii).

رَفته بود he had gone.

(*h*) *Perfect Subjunctive:* mainly confined to subordinate clauses (see (*d*) above and Lessons x–xii).

(*i*) *Future:* used to express the future where the Present (see (*c*) above) would not be sufficiently explicit.

خواهَد رَفت he will go.

69. The Passive

The use of the Passive is generally avoided when any other alternative is possible.

(i) If the doer of the action is expressed, the Active must be used, though the grammatical object may be given the prominence that the Passive gives it in English by bringing it to the beginning of the sentence.

سگ را حَسَن زَد   the dog was beaten by Hasan (lit. Hasan
                          beat the dog).

(ii) If the doer of the action is indefinite or unknown, the impersonal 3rd person *plural* may be used.

سگ را زَدَنَد   the dog was beaten.

(iii) Only where no human or active agent is involved may the Passive be legitimately used.

بِسَبَبِ بَرف راه بَسته شُد   because of the snow the road was
                                 closed.

70. Non-finite Forms

(a) *Past Participle.* In addition to its conjugational use it is frequently found as an adjective, usually *active* in sense.

سال گُذَشته   last year (گُذَشتَن to pass).

پَنجَرۀ شِکَسته   the broken window (شِکَستَن to break).

It may also be used independently as a noun:

گُفته‌هایِ عَلی   the sayings of Ali (گُفتَن to say).

A syntactical use in the construction of complex sentences will be discussed in para. 74.

(b) *Infinitive.* This is used purely as a verbal noun, and cannot be subordinated to a main verb as in English (constructions of this type must be expressed in Persian as subordinate clauses, see para. 75).

The subject or object of an Infinitive verbal noun is linked to it by the *ezafe* construction. In this and all other respects it is treated as an ordinary noun, and may take the suffixes, such as the plural, associated with nouns.

آمَدَنِ حَسَن   Hasan's coming.

خُوردَنِ آب   the drinking of water.

آب ِ خوُردَن   water for drinking, drink-
ing-water.

بَعد از رَفتَن ِ رِضا ماهَم مَنزِل رَفتیم   after Reza's departure (lit.
going), we too went
home.

دیدَنَش مُشکِل اَست   to see him is difficult.

راست نَگُفتَن گُناه است   not to tell the truth (lit.
true) is a sin.

See also para. 86 for another use of the Infinitive.

(c) *Past Stem* (shortened infinitive): used to form the Future with
the Present Tense of خواستَن (see para. 66 above), and also after certain
impersonal verbs (see para. 76).

(d) Other verbal formations will be discussed in para. 99.

71. Irregular Usages

(i) Reference has already been made (para. 65) to the two irregular
Present Tenses of the verb بودَن — رام, ای, است, etc., and هَستَم, هَستی,
هَست, etc. The following peculiarities of this verb should also be noted.

(a) The prefix می... is rarely, if ever, used with the Past Stem. In
other words, there is no distinction between the *Past* and *Imperfect*, both
being rendered by بودَم, etc.

(b) The prefix بِ... is never used with the *Subjunctive* or *Jussive*.

باشَم (that) I may be.

(ii) The following peculiarities are found in the verb داشتَن.

The prefixes می... and بِ... are not used with any of the tenses as
a general rule. Thus the *Past* and *Imperfect* are the same, and also the
Present and *Present Subjunctive*. To avoid confusion in the latter case, the
Perfect Subjunctive is commonly used in place of the *Present Subjunctive*.

داشته باشَم instead دارَم, etc.

However, the prefix می may often be used when داشتَن is the verbal element in a compound verb (see para. 72). This exception does not apply to به.

72. Compound Verbs

One of the most characteristic features of the Persian verbal system is the use of compound verbs. The number of simple verbs is comparatively limited, and the bulk of expressions which in English would be rendered by a simple verb are in Persian rendered by one of a number of common verbs, with the general sense of 'to make', 'to do', 'to have', etc., preceded by a qualifying or distinguishing word, normally a preposition, noun, adjective or adverb. Frequently the 'auxiliary' verb loses much of its normal sense, cf. the use of خوردن in the examples under (a) and (d) below. The following are a few examples:

(a) With Preposition

بَر	up, on.	بَر خوُردَن	meet (by chance).
		بَر داشتَن	pick up.
		بَر گَشتَن	return.
دَر	in.[1]	دَر آمیختَن	mix in, associate.
		دَر آمَدَن	come in (rare; contrast دَر آمَدَن, with opposite meaning, in (d) below).

(b) With Adverb

باز	again, back.	باز کَردَن	open.
		باز گَشتَن	return.
		باز گُفتَن	repeat.
پیش	forward, in front.	پیش رَفتَن	progress.
پَس	behind, back.	پَس دادَن	give back.

[1] Not to be confused with دَر = door (see (d) below).

(c) With Adjective

تَنگ	narrow, tight.	تَنگ کَردَن — tighten.
بیدار	awake.	بیدار کَردَن — waken.
		بیدار شُدَن — awake (intrans.).
بُلَند	tall.	بُلَند کَردَن — raise, erect.
سَوار	mounted.	سَوار کَردَن — mount (trans.).
		سَوار شُدَن — mount (intrans.).
بیرون	outside.	بیرون کردن — expel.
پائین	below.	پائین آوَردَن — lower.
وارِد	entering.	وارِد شُدَن — enter, arrive in.

(d) With Noun

دَر	door.	دَر آمَدن — come out.
		دَر آوَردن — bring out.
صَبر	patience.	صَبر کَردَن — wait.
دوست	friend.	دوست داشتن — like, love.
اِجازه	permission.	اِجازه دادَن — allow.
نِگاه	look, glance.	نِگاه کَردَن — look at.
		نِگاه داشتن — keep, stop.
نِشان	sign.	نِشان دادن — show.
سَرما	cold.	سَرما خوُردَن — catch cold.
زَمِین	ground.	زَمِین خوردَن — fall.
حَرف	word.	حَرف زَدَن — speak.
یاد	memory.	یاد کردن — remember.
		یاد دادن — teach.

The following points are to be noted:

(i) While the non-verbal element is regarded as an integral part of the whole expression, it is separate from the verbal conjugation, and the

E

verbal prefixes, etc., are inserted before the verb itself. However, the prefix بِه is generally omitted.

بَر نَگَشت he did not return.

پیش نَمیرَوَم I am not progressing.

بُلَند میکردند they were raising.

صَبَر خواهَم کَرد I will wait.

صَبَرکُنَد let him wait.

نِشان داده اند they have shown.

(ii) Apart from this, the verbal expression is treated as though it were a single unit, taking a direct object with ...را where appropriate, and so on.

کَمَربَندِ خُود را تَنگ کَرد he tightened his belt.

مُحَمَّد را بیدارکَرد he wakened Mohammed.

Often, when the non-verbal element is an adjective or a noun, a pronominal suffix may be attached to it as the direct object, or even the indirect object.

بیرونَش کَرد he expelled him (= اورا بیرون کَرد).

تَنگَش کَرد he tightened it (= آنرا تَنگ کَرد).

یادَت داد he taught (to) you (= بِتو یاد داد).

This is a somewhat colloquial usage. More literary is the practice of linking the indirect object to the non-verbal element by the *eẓāfe* construction. This is commonly done when the compound verb is an *intransitive* verb formed from a simple verb and an adjective:

سِوارِ آسب شُد he mounted (on) the horse.

واردِ تِهران شُد he arrived in Tehran.

It is sometimes also found when the compound verb is a *transitive* verb formed from a simple verb and a verbal noun.

اِجازهٔ رَفتَن داد he gave permission to go.

A prepositional phrase may also follow the compound element:

یاد از وَطَنِ عَزیزِ خود میکَرد he was recalling his dear homeland.

(iii) The stress tends to pass from the verbal prefix to the non-verbal element of the verbal expression.

Among the commoner 'auxiliary' verbs used in the formation of compound verbs are: کَردَن, to do (often used colloquially in preference to any other); داشتَن to have; گَشتَن, to turn, become; شُدَن, to become; کَشیدَن, to pull; دیدَن, to see.

شُدَن and گَشتَن are commonly used as the passive or intransitive forms of نَمودن, کَردَن, etc., when these occur as part of compound transitive verbs.

It will be seen that often, where in English the verb is the basic form and the noun is formed from it, in Persian the reverse is the case.

إخراج کَردَن	expel.	إخراج	expulsion.
تَشویق کَردَن	encourage.	تَشویق	encouragement.
شِکایَت کَردَن	complain.	شِکایَت	complaint.

In other cases the use of the auxiliary verb with an adjective corresponds to the English causative suffix *-en*.

تَنگ tight.

تَنگ کَردَن tighten.

73. Intonation Patterns

The stress and high pitch falls on the non-verbal part of a compound verb, even when this comes at or near the beginning of the sentence. Where it is widely separated from its verb, there may be a secondary stress on the word immediately preceding the verb.

Para. 69:

sagrɑ ‖ hasan zad

besababe barf ‖ rɑh baste sod

Para. 70:

baʔd az raftane reza ‖ ma ham manzel raftim

didanaš ‖ moškel ast

rast nagoftan ‖ gonah ast

Para. 72:

sabr xaham kard

kamarbande xodra ‖ tang kard

birunaš kard

varede tehran šod

yad az vatane azize xod ‖ mikard

EXERCISES

A. Translate into English:

مِلَّتِ ایران بِشِهادَتِ تاریخ از سُرعَتِ حَرَکَت هَرگِز مَحروم
نَبوده آست. راههای شاهی هَخامَنِشیان اَوَّلین راههای طولانی جَهانِ
مُتَمَدِّن بود. این راهها اُروپا را با آسیا مُتَّصِل ساخت. اَمّا بِطَورِ
کُلّی دَر سابِق مُسافَرَت بَین نُقاطِ دوردَست ایران بَرای عامّهٔ
مَردُم آزیَک تا دو ماه طول کَشید. اِمروز راههای مُتَعَدِّد ساخته
شُد وشَوسههای دَرَجهٔ اَوَّل کوهها را شِکافته آست. مُهِمتَرین
وَسایِلِ جَدید مُسافَرَت دَر ایران کُنونی خَطِّ سَرتاسَری راهِ آهَنِ
ایرانَست. مُسافَرَتِ هَوائی هَم دَر تَمامِ نُقاطِ کِشوَر مُیَسَّر آست.

B. Translate into Persian:

After the death of Alexander the Greek, his empire fell to pieces. In course of time a new Persian dynasty seized the reins of the affairs of the country. This dynasty was known as (by the name of) the Parthians or

Ashkanians. Their capital was in the north of Persia. They fought [for] long years with the Romans, but neither (no) one of (from) the two sides gained a decisive victory. Also commercial and cultural relations between the two empires were many during the reign of the Parthians. Persian life came (became) very much under the influence of Greek culture. The Christian religion gained importance in Persia, and the Persian religion of Mithra became prevalent in the Roman Empire. Nearly six hundred years after the death of Alexander, the Parthian empire was overthrown by Ardashir Papakan (use Active construction), (a) one of the chieftains of the south of Persia. He founded the Sasanid dynasty, and made Persia a great empire once again.

VOCABULARY

nation	ملّت	highway	شوسه
evidence	شهادَت	grade	دَرَجه
speed	سُرعَت	penetrate	شکافتَن
deprived	مَحروم	means (pl. وَسایِل)	وَسیله
royal	شاهی	present-day	کُنونی
first	اَوّلین	line	خَطّ
long	طولانی	end-to-end	سَرتاسَری
world	جَهان	railway	راه آهَن
Europe	اُروبا	Transiranian	سَرتاسَری ایران
join	مُتَّصَل ساختَن (ساز)	aerial	هَوائی
in general	بِطَورِکُلّی	country	کِشوَر
past, former	سابِق	possible	میسَّر
point (pl. نُقاط)	نُقطه	death	وَفات
distant	دوردَست	empire	اِمپِراتوری
generality	عامّه	fall to pieces	بِهَم خوردَن
month	ماه	course	مُرور
last (v.)	طول کَشیدَن	time	زَمان
numerous	مُتَعَدّد	reins	زِمام

affair (pl. أُمُور) آمر

Parthian (pl. پارتها) پارت

Ashkanian آشكانى

capital پایتَخت

north شَمَال

fight جَنگ كَردَن

long years سالِیان دَراز

two sides طَرَفَین

victory پیروزی

decisive قاطِع

gain (victory) یافتَن (یاب)

relation (pl. رَوابِط) رابِطه

commercial تِجارَتی

cultural فَرهَنگی

reign سَلطَنَت

life زَندَگی

influence نُفوذ

culture فَرهَنگ

Greek یونانی

Christian مَسیحی

importance آهَمِّیَت

Mithra میتره

prevalent شایِع

six hundred [see paras. 45 (iii), 88] شِشصَد

overthrow سَرنِگون كَردَن

Ardashir آردَشیر

Papakan پاپَکان

chieftain سالار

south جُنوب

Sasanid ساسانی

found (v.) تأسیس كَردَن

once again بارِدیگَر

LESSON X

Complex Sentences (Co-ordinate, Subordinate).
Impersonal Verbs. Temporal Clauses

74. Co-ordinate Sentences

The simplest form of complex sentence is that in which a number of propositions are linked together by a conjunction such as 'and', 'but', 'or', etc. (see para. 62 above).

نوكَر آمَد و دَررا باز كَرد — The servant came and opened the door.

مَنزِلَم دَرشَهر است، ولی مال شُمادر ییلاق است — My house is in the city, but yours is in the country.

یا کار خود را خوب کُنید، یا منزل   Either do your work well, or go
بِروید   home.

When the actions follow one another in time, the conjunction may often be omitted.

رَفتَم گوشت خریدم   I went [and] bought some meat.

The following idiomatic construction, which is used to emphasize the *continuous action* aspect of the *Present* and *Imperfect*, is an offshoot of the above usage.

دارم آب میخُورم   I am drinking water (lit. I have, I am drinking water).

داشتَم گوشت میخریدم   I was buying meat (lit. I had, I was buying meat).

In a sequence of actions by the same subject (occasionally also by different subjects) all the finite verbs but the last may be replaced by the Past Participle. The conjunction 'and' is optional in this case.

حَسَن بِشَهر آمده (و) بِسینما رفت   Hasan came to town and went to the cinema.

This construction may be used even when the time of the actions is in the future.

فَردا بشهر رَفته (و) گوشت خواهم   Tomorrow I shall go to the town
خرید   and buy some meat.

When compound verbs are used, the verbal element of all but the last may be omitted, the element in the last verb being taken to apply to all. This practice is permissible even when different verbal elements would be required for each compound verb in the sentence, or even when the last verb is not compound.

حَسَن وارد اُطاق (شُده) وخِیلی   Hasan entered the room and
عَصَبانی شُد   became very angry.

حسن وارد اطاق (شده) و صدا زَد   Hasan entered the room and called out.

حسن وارد اطاق (شده) وشام خورُد   Hasan entered the room and ate supper.

Similarly the verb 'to be' may be omitted except in the *last* of a series of parallel sentences.

در تهران خیابانها پهن، عمارتها بلند، ومغازه ها متعدّد است.	In Tehran the streets are wide, the houses tall, and the shops numerous.

75. Subordinate Sentences

When the second action is in some way dependent on the first, or arising out of it, as a result of a wish, purpose, command, obligation, remembering, forgetting, fear, decision, request, etc., the two clauses may be placed in juxtaposition as in para. 74, without a conjunction, and the subordinate verb is put in the Subjunctive. It is important to note that the Infinitive can *never* be used for this type of construction.

بشهر میروم گوشت بخرم	I am going to the town to buy meat (lit. . . . [that] I may buy meat).
میخواهم منزل بروم	I wish to go home.
میل دارم با او آشنا شوم	I would like to become acquainted with him.
امید دارم شما را زود ببینم	I hope to see you soon.

The tense of the subordinate verb is (in all types of subordinate sentence) related to the time of the main action; that is to say, if the subordinate action is subsequent to the main action, the subordinate verb is put in the *Present*, whatever the tense of the main verb may be.

بشهر رفتم گوشت بخرم	I went to the town to buy meat (lit. I went to the town [that] I may buy meat).
نمیتوانستم مهمانخانهٔ خوبی پیدا کنم	I was unable to find a good hotel.
باو آمر داد دفتر را بیاورد	He ordered him to bring the account book.
آزاو خواهش کردند اطاق را ترک کنند	They asked him to leave the room.

76. Impersonal Verbs

A number of impersonal verbs and expressions with the sense of obligation, possibility, and so on, are followed by the *Subjunctive*. The commonest include the defective verb بایِستَن, 'to be necessary', which is only found in current Persian in the 3rd Person Singular of the *Present* and *Past* Tenses (both without prefix): بایَد 'it is necessary'; بایِست, 'it was necessary'; and phrases like میشَوَد، مُمکِن اَست, 'it is possible'; قِرارشُد (میشَوَد), 'it was (is) agreed'; کافی اَست, 'it is sufficient'; All these expressions may also be used in the past tense.

بایَد هَرچِه زودتَر بِرَوید	You must go at once (lit. it is necessary [that] you may go as quickly as possible).
آیا مُمکِن اَست (میشَوَد) فَردا بیائید؟	Is it possible for you to come to-morrow?
قِرار شُد اینجا بِمانیم	It was agreed that we stay here.
خوب بود اینجا زِندَگی کُنید	It was good for you to live here.
نَبایِست بیایَد	He ought not to have come.

Sometimes, by putting the subordinate verb in the *Imperfect* (see also para. 85 for the use of the Imperfect to express a past action that did not in fact take place), the idea is conveyed of an action that might or should have been carried out, but was not.

بایَد آن مَردرا میدیدید	You should have seen that man.
خوب بود اینجا زِندَگی میکَردید	It would have been good for you to live here.

Certain adverbial expressions may take the place of the main verb.

کاش (کاشکه) این را میدیدید	Would that you had seen this!

When بایِست is used to introduce a clause of this kind, it generally carries the otherwise obsolete Imperfect verbal suffix بایِستی : ....ی (not to be confused with the 2nd Person Singular).

بایِستی بِرَوَم	I ought to have gone (but I didn't).

If it is desired to express a general obligation, possibility, etc., in which the subordinate verb has no subject, the *Past Stem* (shortened infinitive) is used instead of the *Present Subjunctive*.

بایَد رفت	One ought to go.
بایِست گُفت	One had to say, it had to be said.
بایِستی گُفت	One ought to have said (but didn't).
مُمکِن است (میشَوَد) رفت	It is possible to go.

The verb تَوانِستَن 'to be able' may also be used in this impersonal construction, in which case it loses its personal ending in the *Present Tense*.

میتَوان رفت	It is possible to go.
میتُوانِست گُفت	It was possible to say.

Contrast

میتَوانَد بِرَوَد	He can go.
میتوانِست بگویَد	He could have said.

The defective verb شایَد (lit. 'it is suitable') has virtually lost its verbal identity, and is generally used as a simple adverb with the meaning 'perhaps'.

شایَد فردا میرَوَم	Perhaps I will go tomorrow.
شایَد آنجانَبود	Perhaps he was not there.

If, however, it is desired to emphasize the uncertainty of the action, the *Subjunctive* (*Present* or *Perfect*) may be used. This usage is also applicable to adverbs or adverbial expressions of similar meaning with no verbal element.

شاید آنجا نَباشد	Perhaps he will (lit. may) not be there.
بِخیالَم آنجا نباشد	I imagine (lit. in my imagination) he will not be there.
بَلکه بمیرد	Perhaps he will (lit. may) die.

77. The Conjunction که

With the exception of those governed by an Impersonal Verb and using the Shortened Infinitive (para. 76), most of the above subordinate clauses may be linked to the main sentence by the conjunction که 'that' without any other change.

بشهر میرَوَم که گوشت بِخَرَم	I am going to the town to buy meat.
خوب بود که اینجا زندگی کنید	It was good for you to live here.
باو امر داد که دفتر را بیاوَرد	He ordered him to bring the account book.
از او خواهش کردند که اُطاق را تَرک کُنَد	They asked him to leave the room.

The conjunction که has a very wide range of uses. In general it serves to indicate a dependent relationship between a sentence, phrase, or single word, and a subordinate clause. It can never by itself begin a sentence.

78. Indirect Statements

Clauses dependent on verbs such as 'say, think, believe, feel, agree, know, ask', etc., are introduced by the conjunction که, and frequently remain in the same form as in the direct speech, that is to say, neither person nor tense of the verb are changed.

گفت که بشهر میروَم	He said that he was going to the town (lit. . . . .that I am going to the town).

Alternatively, the person may be changed (to the 3rd), but *not* the tense (see para. 75).

گفت که بشهر میرَوَد	He said that he was going to the town (lit. . . . .that he is going to the town).

Further examples:

آیا میدانید که این صَحیح است یانه؟	Do you know whether this is true or not?
خیال میکنُم که اِشتِباه کرده اید	I think that you have made a mistake.

پُرسید که چِطور میتَوانَم ببازار بِرَسَم

He asked how he could reach the bazaar.

سُؤال کرد که این کتابرا کُجا پیدا کَردی

He asked where he found this book (lit. . . .that—this book where did you find?).

تَعَجُّب میکردم که این مَرد کُجا وچطور زندگی میکُنَد

I wondered where and how this man lived.

Frequently the verb 'to say' may be omitted and implied in the conjunction:

نَوکَر آمد که آربابم اینجا نیست

The servant came to say that his master was not there (lit. the servant came that my master is not here).

79. Temporal and other Dependent Clauses

The conjunction که is also used to introduce what are really main sentences set in a point of time or place, a cause, etc., this being determined by the grammatical main sentence.

Time:

عَصر بود که وارِدِ شَهر شُدیم

It was evening when (lit. that) we reached the city.

مُدَّتی است که شما را نَدیدَم

It is a [long] time since I have seen you (lit. that I have not seen you).

روزی در شَهر بودَم که باحَسَن بَرخوردَم

I was in the town one day when I ran into Hasan.

Place:

در اصفَهان بود که دَفعهٔ اوَّل آن شَخص را دیدم

It was in Isfahan that I first saw that person.

Cause:

طَوری شکایَت کرد که ناچار اورا اِخراج کَردند

He complained so much (lit. [in] a manner) that they were obliged to discharge him (lit. necessarily they dismissed him).

چُنان تَنبل بود که تاظهر بیدار نشد   He was so lazy that he did not wake up till noon.

طوفان سَبَبِ این شُد که خانه ویران گَشت   The storm was the cause of this house being destroyed (lit. that the house became destroyed).

Comparison:

مِثلِ این بود که هرگز نیامَد   It was as if he had never come.

In the above examples the verb of the 'subordinate' clause expresses an accomplished fact. Where it refers to a future or unlikely action, the *Subjunctive* is used.

این طَناب آنقَدر مُحکَم نیست که آن باررا بِکَشَد   This rope is not strong enough to pull that load (lit. . . .is not so strong that it may pull that load).

In all these examples the conjunction could be omitted.

It will be seen that in each case the grammatical main sentence precedes the subordinate clause, and in fact is prior to it in time. Where the reverse is the case, a different construction must be used (see paras. 81, 82).

79a. Intonation Patterns

In complex sentences the standard pattern is a rising intonation for the first clause (whether this is the main or subordinate clause) and a falling intonation for the second. However, there may often be a 'peak' in the second part represented by a verbal prefix or some other usually stressed word.

Para. 74:

noukar ɑmad o ‖ darrɑ bɑz kɑrd

manzelam dar sahr ast ‖ vali mɑle šomɑ dar yilɑq ast

yɑ kɑre xodrɑ xub konid ‖ yɑ manzel beravid

dɑram ɑb mixoram

hasan bešahr ɑmade (o) ‖ besinema raft

fardɑ bešahr rafte (o) ‖ gušt xɑham xarid

Para. 75:

bešahr miravam ‖ gušt bexaram

meil daram baʔu ‖ ašna šavam

namitavanestam ‖ mehmanxaneye xubi peida konam

beʔu amr dad ‖ daftarra beyavarad

az u xaheš kardand ‖ otaqra tark konad

Para. 76:

bayad harce zudtar beravid

aya momken ast ‖ farda beyaʔid?

xub bud ‖ inja zandagi konid

bayad an mardra mididid

kaš(ke) inra mididid

šayad farda miravam

Para. 78:

goft ke ‖ besahr miravam

aya midanid ke ‖ in sahih ast ya na

xeyal mikonam ke ‖ eštebah kardeʔid

porsid ke ‖ cetour mitavanam ‖ bebazar berasam

suʔal kard ke ‖ in ketabra ‖ koja peida kardi

taʔajjob mikardam ke ‖ in mard ‖ koja va cetour

zandagi mikonad

Para. 79:

$$\text{asr bud ke} \parallel \text{varede šahr šodim}$$

$$\text{touri šekayat kard ke} \parallel \text{nacar} \parallel \text{ura exraj kardand}$$

$$\text{mesle in bud ke} \parallel \text{hargez nayamad}$$

$$\text{in tanab} \parallel \text{anqadr mohkam nist ke} \parallel \text{an barra bekašad}$$

EXERCISES

A. Translate into English:

آب و هوای ایران

ایران در مَنطَقهٔ مُعتَدِل شمالی قراردارد وبِدین سَبَب آب وهَوای
آن بِطَور کُلّی مُعتَدِل است، امّا بِعلّتِ کوههای بُلند وگُستَرده
وصَحراهای پَهناوَر ومُجاورتِ دریاها، انواع گوناگونِ آب وهوای مُعتَدِل
در آن میبینیم. درکِنارههای دریای مازَندَران آب وهوا معتدل، در صحراهایِ
داخِلی گَرم و خُشک، در کوهِستانها سرد، و درکِنارههای جنوب
بسیارگرم است. بارانیترین جایِ ایران کِنارههایِ دریایِ مازَندَران،
وخُشکترین ناحیهٔ آن کَویرِ لوت است.

B. Translate into Persian:

In the history of Persia its climate has had much influence. In the prehistoric period it is said that the central plateau was a great internal sea, and men first lived in caves in the mountains. Gradually the sea became dry, and its shores turned into rich farm-lands. But in the course of time the land became even dryer, and already by (until) the Middle Ages a great part of the country was desert. In these districts farming could only be carried out by means of irrigation, and that is still the greatest problem in Persia at the present time. Important new irrigation schemes are being carried out north of Tehran, near Isfahan, on the Safidrud (White River) in Gilan, and in other parts of the country.

VOCABULARY

zone منطقه

temperate معتدل

northern شمالی

be situated قرار داشتن

climate آب و هَوا

widespread گُسترده

desert صحرا

extensive پهناوَر

nearness مُجاوَرَت

sea دَریا

kind, sort (pl. انواع) نَوع

various گوناگون

shore کناره

Mazandaran مازندَران

rainy بارانی

internal داخِلی

mountainous area کوهستان

district (pl. نَواحی) ناحیه

salt desert کَویر

Lut لوت

prehistoric قَبل از تاریخ

plateau فَلات

cave غار

gradually رَفته رَفته

turn into ... به (گَرد–) گَشتن

rich (fertile) حاصلخیز

farm-land (pl. مَزارِع) مَزرَعه

even هَم

already هَم اکنون

Middle Ages [1] قُرونِ وُسطَی

desert بیابان

farming زراعَت

carry out اجرا کَردَن

irrigation آبیاری

problem مُشکِل

scheme طَرح

Safidrud سَفیدرود

Gilan گیلان

LESSON XI

Complex Sentences (*cont.*) (Relative Clauses)

80. Relative Clauses

The term 'Relative Clause' is used here to describe a range of complex sentences, only one group of which may be rendered in English by clauses introduced by the pronouns 'who, which', etc.

---

[1] See para. 57 (note).

(a) Temporal

In these sentences the time of the whole complex is determined by the verb of the main sentence. The verb of the subordinate clause, which is introduced by a noun (not necessarily the subject), adverb, adjective, etc., followed by که, is therefore normally in the past, and indicates an action or circumstance arising before the action of the main verb.

کارمان که تمام شد منزل رفتیم	When our work was finished, we went home (lit. our work that it was finished . . .).
کارمان که تمام شد منزل میرویم	When our work is finished, we will go home.
زمستان که آمد سرد میشود	When winter comes, it will be cold (lit. winter that it came . . .).
نزدیک که علی آمد اورا شناختم	When Ali came near, I recognized him (lit. near that Ali came . . .).
سوار اتوبوس که شدیم رضارا دیدیم	When we had boarded the bus, we saw Reza (lit. mounted on the bus that we became . . .).

The last two sentences could also be rendered, with a slight change of emphasis, as follows:

علی که نزدیک آمد اورا شناختم	When Ali came near, I recognized him (lit. Ali that he came near . . .).
ماکه سوار اتوبوس شدیم رضارا دیدیم	When we had boarded the bus, we saw Reza (lit. we that we became mounted on the bus . . .).

In these last examples the emphasis is on the doers of the action rather than the place or circumstances.

شماکه باین زودی میروید (or رفتید) کَی برمیگردید؟	Now that you are going (lit. You, that you are going) so soon, when will you return?
از سخنان این اشخاص که فریفته شد، تقاضاها یشان را قبول کرد	Because he was deceived by the words of these people he accepted their demands.

(b) Appositional

These are similar to the last three examples, but there is no time element involved. Often the main verb may precede the subordinate clause.

این مَرد که دوستِ من میباشد شما را راهنَمائی خواهد کرد	This man, who is my friend (lit. that he is my friend), will guide you.
آقای دُکتُر که اِمروز نَیامَد اینجا نیست	The doctor is not here, for he did not come today.
پیر مَردی با زَن وبَچّه وارد شدکه تَمامِ لباسَش پاره شُد	An old man with a wife and child came in, all of whose clothes were torn (lit. that all his clothes were torn).
حَسَن عَموئی داشت که دو سال بود زَنَش دَر گُذَشته است	Hasan had an uncle whose wife had passed away two years previously (lit. .... that it was two years his wife has passed away).

(c) Selective or Determinative

The following examples come nearest to the Relative Clause as understood in English, in that the clause selects or in some way determines one unit or a group from a general class. There is, however, no relative pronoun in Persian, and the construction is similar to that in (b) above, with two important distinctions:

(i) The antecedent is identified by the addition of the suffix ی ... (not to be confused with the Indefinite suffix). This suffix is unstressed. (For rules governing its orthography after nouns ending in a vowel see para. 39 A(ii).)

(ii) The conjunction که must follow the antecedent immediately, only the particle را ... being interpolated when this is required. This is the main feature, other than the context, that enables the *selective* relative clause to be distinguished from the *appositional*, when the antecedent to the latter is an indefinite noun with the indefinite suffix ی (see the last two examples in (b) above).

In all cases the subordinate clause must contain a pronoun, expressed or implied, referring back to the antecedent. This of course is frequently the subject of the subordinate verb, and therefore not expressed separately; it may also be omitted where there is no possible ambiguity, for instance, when it is the direct object of the subordinate verb.

The following table sets out the different types of Selective Relative Clause that may occur:

Main sentence	Relative Clause	Pronoun	Conj.	...ra	Suffix	Antecedent
	دیروز آمَد	[او]				A1
اینجاست	دیروز دیدید	(اورا)	که	—	ی	مَرد 2
	هَدیه دادید	باو				3
	دیروز آمَد	[او]				B1
اِمروز دیدَم	دیروز دیدید	(اورا)	که	را	ی	مرد 2
	هَدیه دادید	باو				3
	دیروز آمد	[او]				C1
حَرف زَدَم	دیروز دیدید	(اورا)	که	—	ی	بامرد 2
	هدیه دادید	باو				3

In the first group the Antecedent is the *subject* of the *main verb*, in the second the *direct object*, and in the third the *indirect object*. Similarly in each group the three examples show the antecedent as subject, direct object, and indirect object of the *subordinate verb*. In all cases it will be seen that the subordinate clause is in such a form that it could stand by itself without alteration.

Translation:

A1.	The man		who came yesterday	is here
		(lit. that	[he] came yesterday)	
2.	The man		whom you saw yesterday	is here
		(lit. that	you saw (him) yesterday)	
3.	The man		to whom you gave a present	is here
		(lit. that	you gave to him a present)	
B1.	The man		who came yesterday	I saw today
2.	The man		whom you saw yesterday	I saw today
3.	The man		to whom you gave a present	I saw today
C1.	With the man		who came yesterday	I spoke
2.	With the man		whom you saw yesterday	I spoke
3.	With the man		to whom you gave a present	I spoke

In addition to the omission of the pronoun in the subordinate clause, already referred to, idiomatic usages also often occur when the antecedent has one status in the main sentence and another in the subordinate clause. In such cases the influence of the subordinate clause, coming first, may out-balance that of the main sentence.

(i) In example B1, where the antecedent is the object of the main sentence but the subject of the subordinate clause, the particle را . . . may be omitted.

مَردی که دیروز آمد اِمروز دیدم

(ii) In example A2, where the antecedent is the subject of the main sentence but the object of the subordinate clause, the pronoun in the subordinate clause is omitted, but the particle را . . . is transferred to the antecedent itself, even though this is not permitted by the structure of the main sentence.

مَردی را که دیروز دیدید اینجاست

A similar usage occurs more rarely in example A3.

بِمَردی که هَدیه دادید اینجاست

In normal practice this last only happens when there is a considerable separation between the antecedent and the main verb.

با زبانیکه ما اِمروز سُخَن میگوئیم وآنرا فارسی نِسبَت میدهیم هَمان زَبانی است که هِزار سال پیش رَواج داشت

The language (with) which we speak today and which we call Persian is the same language that was current a thousand years ago.

The antecedent may be qualified by an adverb or adjective, especially a superlative or adjective of quantity.

<div dir="rtl">تَنها کَسی که اینجابود مَن بودَم</div>	The only person (who was) here was I.
<div dir="rtl">بِهترین چیزیکه در مَنزِلِ من است این قالی است</div>	The best thing (that is) in my house is this carpet.
<div dir="rtl">تَمامِ کارگرانیکه اِعتِصاب کردَند امروز برگشتند</div>	All the workers who were on strike returned today.

In the following construction the verb 'to be' is inserted between the antecedent and the conjunction.

تنها کسی است که بآن مملکت رفته است
He is the only person who has been to that country.

بهترین کتابی است که تابحال خواندم
It is the best book that I have read up to now.

81. Adverbial Conjunctions

A modification of the Relative construction is used in the formation of a large number of adverbial and prepositional expressions that serve as conjunctions of time, place, purpose, cause, etc. The following are a few examples. In each case the expression consists of a noun (often governed by a preposition) bearing the suffix ی . . . and followed by the conjunction که.

Time: وَقتیکه when (lit. at the time that).

تا وقتیکه as long as (lit. until the time that).

آز وقتیکه since (lit. from the time that).

دَر حالیکه while (lit. in the condition that).

Locative: (دَر) جائیکه where.

Causal: آز آنجائیکه because (lit. from that place that).

Concessive: در حالیکه whereas (lit. in the condition that).

با وُجودیکه in spite of the fact that (lit. with the existence that).

Comparative: تاحَدّیکه، بِطَوریکه، هَمانطَوریکه to the extent that, just as.

Consecutive: تا حَدّیکه، بِطَوریکه so that, to such an extent that.

Examples:

وقتیکه رَسیدم دَربَسته شُد
When I arrived, the door was closed.

از وقتیکه آمد خَیلی سرد بود
Since he came, it has been very cold.

در جائیکه شهر بود فَقَط بیابان
است

Where the city was, there is only desert.

همانطوریکه گفتند رفتار میکرد

He acted just as they had said.

از آنجائیکه خَسته بود رفت خوابید

Because he was tired, he went to bed (lit. he went, slept).

با وُجودیکه گُرُسنه بود کار خودرا
تمام کرد

Although he was hungry, he finished his work.

کفشهای خودرا واکس کرد بطوریکه
بَرق میزَد

He polished his shoes so that they shone.

Sometimes the که may be separated from the noun or prepositional phrase.

وقتی لیوان را بزمین گُذاشت که یك
قطره آب در آن نبود

He [only] put down (lit. on the ground) the glass when there was not a drop of water in it.

Another way of expressing the comparative idea involves the use of the compound conjunction ازبَسکه, 'inasmuch as' (lit. from enough that).

از بسکه فریاد زد مردم خسته شدند

He shouted so much that (lit. inasmuch as he shouted) people became tired.

82. Prepositional Conjunctions

Subordinate clauses may be introduced by prepositions through the interpolation of the pronouns آن or این and the conjunction که.

Time: پیش (قَبَل) از آنکه — before.

پَس (بَعد) از آنکه — after.

دَر ضِمنِ اینکه — while (lit. in the contents of this that).

تا اینکه — until, as long as.

Purpose: بَرای اینکه — in order that.

Comparison: مثل اینکه — as if.

چُنانکه (چون آنکه for) — just as.

Cause: بِعِلَّتِ اینکه   because.

Concessive: با (وُجودِ) اینکه   although.

مَگَر اینکه   unless.

Consecutive: تا اینکه   so that (with Subjunctive).

Examples:

بَعد از آنکه حسن رفته بود مُحَمَّد وارد شُد

After Hasan had gone, Mohammad entered.

بَرای اینکه اشتباه نَشَوَد در دَفتَر نَوِشت

In order that there might be no mistake, he wrote (it) in the register.

از اُطاقِ خارج شد مِثلِ اینکه او را نشنید

He went out of the room as if he had not heard him.

بِعِلَّتِ اینکه هَواپیَما دیر آمد نَمیتَوانِست در جَلَسه شِرکَت کُنَد

Because the plane was late, he was unable to take part in the meeting.

با اینکه سَخت باران بُود فَوراً راه اُفتاد

Although it was raining hard, he started out at once.

سَخت کار میکرد تا اینکه از اِمتِحان خوب گُذَرَد

He worked hard so as to pass the examination well (verb in the Subjunctive because the action was not completed at the time of the main action).

چُنانکه میبینید این اُطاق بُزُرگتر است

As you see, this room is larger.

Comparative sentences may also be formed by using the comparative adjective and از followed by آن که.

این دَرس آسانتر از آن است که تَصَوُّر کردید

This lesson is easier than (that that) you imagined.

او باهوشتَر از آن است که این حکایت را باوَر کُنَد

He is too clever to believe (cleverer than that that he would believe) this story.

Other expressions using این or آن and که include:

همین که، همانکه، همین طورکه   just when, at that same time as.

چندانکه   as long as, as much as.

وحال آنکه   whereas.

When the action in the subordinate clause is earlier in time than that of the main clause, the subordinate verb is put in the Past or Pluperfect, even though the time of both actions relative to the speaker may be future. Similarly, when the subordinate action is later in time than the main action, the subordinate verb will normally be in the Subjunctive, even though both actions may be past relative to the speaker.

بعد از آنکه حسن رفت، من هم
خواهم رفت

After Hasan goes, I too will go.

قبل از آنکه برسد، کار تمام شد

Before he arrived, the work was finished.

Subordinate clauses introduced by a compound conjunction are generally placed before the main clause. Thus the choice lies between a subordinate clause introduced by a compound conjunction and (generally) *preceding* the main clause (paras. 81, 82), and one introduced by a simple که and following the main clause (para. 79). This choice may perhaps best be clarified by saying that که implies some undefined relationship between the two clauses. Where the context of the clauses makes the relationship clear, که is sufficient (though a more complex conjunctional expression may of course be used if desired); where there is a possibility of ambiguity, a conjunction specifying the relationship should be employed.

Thus:

زمستان که آمد سرد میشود   When winter comes, it will be cold.

means much the same as:

وقتیکه زمستان آمد سرد میشود

But

گرسنه که بود کار خود را تمام کرد

could mean: When he was hungry, he finished his work.

or: Because he was hungry, . . .

or even: Although he was hungry, . . .

On the other hand there is no ambiguity about

با وجودیکه گرسنه بود کار خود را تمام کرد

which can only mean: Although he was hungry, he finished his work.

83. Pronominal Conjunctions

The pronouns این and آن may be used relatively with the conjunction که, and without the addition of the relative suffix ی . . .

آنکه بُلَندتراست پیش بیایَد Let him who is tallest come forward.

آنکه is generally used only for animate beings; for inanimate objects the correct expression is آنچه که, though the که is frequently omitted.

آنچه (که) دَر کِتاب است راست است What is in the book is true.

آنچه may take the suffix را . . . when it is the object of the main verb (and also idiomatically when it is the object of the subordinate verb, cf. para. 80(c) (ii)). In this case the conjunction که must be retained.

آنچه (راکه) گفت راست است What he said is true.

آنچه may also be used with prepositions and prepositional expressions.

باوُجودِ آنچه گفت خواهَم رَفت In spite of what he said, I shall go.

The form چُنانچه [which must not be confused with چُنانکه (see para. 82)] is used to introduce a future or doubtful proposition, and has therefore acquired almost the meaning of 'if' (other conditional clauses are dealt with in para. 85).

چُنانچه صلاح بدانید فَردا حَرَکت میکنیم If you think fit, we shall leave tomorrow.

83a. Intonation Patterns

Sentences of the para. 80(a) and (b) types tend to have a secondary peak immediately before the که and a primary peak on the subordinate verb. In the Selective Relative Clauses (paras. 80 (c) and 81) there is a secondary stress on the antecedent. A similar pattern is observable in para. 82.

Para. 80(*a*):

karaman ke tamam šod ‖ manzel raftim

sevare otubus ke šodim ‖ rezara didim

ma ke sevare otubus šodim ‖ rezara didim

az soxanane in ašxas ke farifte šod ‖ taqazahayašanra ‖ qabul

kard

(*b*):

in mard ‖ ke duste man mibašad ‖ šomara rahnamaʔi xahad

kard

pire mardi ‖ ba zan o bacce vared šod ‖ ke tamame lebasaš ‖

pare šod

hasan amuʔi dašt ‖ ke do sal bud ‖ zanaš dar gozašte ast

(*c*):

mardike diruz amad ‖ injast

Para. 81:

vaqtike rasidam ‖ dar baste šod

dar jaʔike šahr bud ‖ faqat biyaban ast

kafšhaye xodra vaks kard ‖ betourike barq mizad

vaqti livanra bezamin gozašt ke ‖ yak qatre ab ‖ dar an nabud

in dars asantar az an ast ke ‖ tasavvor kardid

in bahuštar az an ast ke ‖ in hekayatra ‖ bavar konad

Para. 82:

baʔd az ɑn ke hasan rafte bud ‖ mohammad vɑred šod

barɑye inke eštebɑh našavad ‖ dar daftar navešt

beʔellate inke havɑpeimɑ dir ɑmad ‖ namitavɑnest dar jalase

    šerkat konad

saxt kɑr kard tɑ inke ‖ az emtehɑn xub gozarad

conɑnke mibinid ‖ in otɑq bozorgtar ast

Para. 83:

ɑnke bolandtar ast ‖ piš beyɑyad

ɑnce ke dar ketɑbast ‖ rɑst ast

bɑ vojude ɑnce goft ‖ xɑham raft

conɑnce salɑh bedɑnid ‖ fardɑ harakat mikonam

EXERCISES

A. Translate into English:

نجاتِ ماه

شبِ مَهتابی مُلّا دَر چاه نِگاه میکرد عَکسِ ماه را در چاه دید. فِکرکَرد که ثَواب دارد ماهرا از چاه نِجات دِهَد. پَس قُلّابی درچاه اَنداخته چَند دَور گَردانید. از قَضا قُلّاب بِسَنگِ بُزُرگی دَر تَهِ چاه گیرکَرد. مُلّا خیلی سَعی کرد آنرا بالا بِکَشد آمّا ازجای خَود تکان نَخورد. زیاد قُوَّت کرد ریسمان پاره شُد مُلّا بِپُشت اُفتاد. نِگاه کرد ماه را در آسْمان دید گُفت: عَیب نَدارد خیلی رَنج کَشیدَم بِمَقصَد رَسیده ماه را نِجات دادم.

B. Translate into Persian:

   With the victory of Ardashir Papakan a new period began for Persia.
The Zoroastrian faith was established once again as the national faith of
Persia, and the government and the religious leaders worked sincerely
together. As a result a strong centralized government was established,
which encouraged feelings of patriotism and nationalism among the
people. Among (from) the famous personalities of this period were
Shapur I, who humbled the Roman Emperor Valerian; Shapur the Great,
who reigned for seventy years and strengthened and expanded the empire;
Nushirvan the Just, who revived the administration and codified laws;
and the prophet Mani, who founded a religion that was rejected in Persia
itself, but spread widely in Europe and central Asia.

VOCABULARY

moonlit	مَهتابی	try	سَعی کَردَن
well	چاه	move (intr.)	تَکان خوُردَن
look	نِگاه کَردَن	force (v.)	قوُّت کَردَن
reflection	عَکس	cord	ریسمان
think	فِکرکَردَن	break (intr.)	پاره شُدَن
that (conj.)	که	sky	آسمان
spiritual reward	ثَواب	never mind!	عَیب نَدارَد
rescue	نِجات دادَن	take trouble	رَنج کَشیدَن
hook	قُلّاب	intention	مَقصَد
throw	آنداختَن (آنداز)	arrive	رَسیدَن
turn (n.)	دَور	begin	شُروع کَردَن
spin (v.)	گَردانیدَن	Zoroastrian	زَردُشتی
by chance	آز قَضا	be established	بَرقِرار شُدَن
stone	سَنگ	as	بِرَسم
bottom	تَه	government	دَولَت
get caught	گیر کَردَن	religious leader	روُحانی (روُحانیین .pl)

together	باهَم	seventy [see paras. 45 (iii), 88] هَفتاد	
work (v.)	كار كَردَن	reign (v.)	سَلطَنَت كَردَن
sincere	صَمیمانه	strengthen	مُحكَم كَردَن
as a result	دَر نَتیجه	expand	تَوسعه دادَن
centralized	مُتَمَركَز	encourage	تَشویق كَردَن
Nushirvan	نوشیروان		
feeling (pl. إحساسات)	حِسّ	just (adj.)	عادِل
patriotism	وَطَن دوستی	administration	حُكومَت
nationalism	مِلَّت پَرَستی	revive	قُوَّت دادَن
personality		law (pl. قَوانین)	قانون
شَخصِیَّت (شَخصِیَّتها .pl)		codify	تَدوین كَردَن
Shapur	شاپور	Mani	مانی
emperor	اِمپِراطور	reject	رَدّ كَردَن
Valerian	والیریان	spread	رَواج یافتَن
humble (v.)	تَحقیر كَردَن	widely	زیاد

LESSON XII

Complex Sentences (*cont.*)
(Indefinite Relative.   Other Conjunctions.
Conditional Sentences)

84. Indefinite Relative Conjunctions

The word هَر 'each' is used to form a variety of conjunctions from pronouns and other words, giving them the sense of the English '-ever'.

هركَسیكه، هَر آنكه، هَركه   whoever.

هرآنچه (كه)، هرچه (كه)   whatever.

The following do not take كه

هركَس   whoever.

هر کُدام	whichever
هر وقت، هرگاه	whenever.
هر جا، هرکُجا	wherever.
هرطَور، هرقَدر، هرچَند	however.

هرچند often has the sense of 'although'.

Since such expressions are by their nature doubtful or indefinite, they are normally followed by the verb in the *Subjunctive*, unless it refers to an action that has already happened in relation to the main verb.

هرکه باشد، مَیل دارم اورا ببینَم	Whoever he is, I should like to see him.
هرکه را آنجادیدی بِمَنزلِ من بیاوَر	Bring anyone you see there to my house.
هر که (را) آنجاباشد (بود) بمنزلِ من بیاوَر	Bring anyone who is there to my house.
هرچه (راکه) زیادی داشتند فُروختند	Whatever they had in excess, they sold.
هر کُدام ازاینها را لازم داری بگیر	Take whichever of these you need.
هروقت اینجا آمدید هَوا بَد است	Whenever you come here the weather is bad.
هرجا میرَوَد باخوشحالی اِستِقبال میکنند	Wherever he goes, he is welcomed with pleasure (lit. they (impers.) welcome [him] with pleasure).
هرچند اصرارکُنی قَبول نَمیکنم	However you insist, I shall not agree.
هرطَوری بود، بِهَترطور بود، هرطور شده	somehow or other.

The use of هرچه with the comparative adjective has already been mentioned (para. 45 (i)). The following construction should be noted.

هرچه زودتر (sc. باشد) بِهتَر (خواهد بود .sc)	the sooner the better.

84a. Other Conjunctions

A small number of words, mostly prepositional in origin, are commonly used as conjunctions without the interpolation of any other particle, though که may often be added.

(a) چون 'when'. In this sense it never takes the conjunction که.

چون داخل اطاق شد مَنظَرَهٔ غَریبی دید
When he entered the room, he saw a strange sight.

(b) چه (که)، زیرا (که)، چون (که) 'since, because'. All these may be used with or without که. چه generally only introduces a subordinate clause *following* the main clause.

چون درآن شهر آشنائی نـداشت بمهمانخانه رفت
Since he had no acquaintances in that town, he went to an hotel.

کارم راتمام نَکردم چه میخواستم تآتر بروَم
I did not finish my work, because I wished to go to the theatre.

(c) The conjunction تا has a variety of allied meanings.

(i) 'as long as', 'as far as', 'as much as'.

تا اینجا هَستید باید کُمَک کنید
As long as you are here, you must help.

تا چشم کارمیکرد جُزکوه وجنگَل هیچ نبود
As far as the eye could see (lit. worked), there was nothing but mountain and forest.

تا بتوانی راست بگو
Tell the truth as far as you can.

(ii) 'as soon as', 'by the time that' (depending on the tense of the following verb).

تا اینجا برگَشتید بشما نشان خواهم داد
As soon as you return here, I will show you.

تا حَرَکت کنید حاضر خواهیم شد
By the time you leave, we shall be ready.

(iii) 'until' (normally followed by the verb in the negative).

تا قبول نکردید هیچی نخواهم گفت
I shall say nothing until you agree.

(iv) 'in order that' (with verb in Subjunctive).

صبحِ زود حرکت کرد تاعَصر بِرسَد

He left early in the morning in order to arrive by evening.

تا is sometimes used in this sense after verbs of command, etc.

امرداد تا زود حرکت کند

He ordered him to set out early.

Often the subordinate verb is put in the Past Tense, in which case the two meanings under (iii) and (iv) are combined.

امرداد تا زود حرکت کرد

He ordered him to set out early (and he did).

(v) 'than' (in comparisons between two actions or verbal ideas).

با هوشترَید تایکچنین کاری بکنید

You are too sensible to do such a thing.

بِهتر است اینجا بمانیم تا دراین هوا بیرون رویم

It is better for us to stay here than to go out in this weather.

Often the second verb may be omitted.

رضا زرنگتَر است تا مُحَمَّد

Reza is cleverer than Mohammad (is).

با هواپیما زودترمیرسی تابا اُتوبوس

You will get there sooner by plane than by bus.

85. Conditional Sentences

The protasis ('if' clause) in Conditional Sentences is introduced normally by the conjunction اَگَر (with or without کِه). The tenses of the verb in protasis and apodosis are determined by the nature of the condition, which may be possible or impossible. (For the use of چُنانچه in a similar construction see para. 82.)

(a) *Possible*. The protasis verb is in the *Subjunctive* (*Present* or *Perfect*), the apodosis verb in the *Present* or *Future*.

اَگَر اِجازه بِدهید حالا میرَوَم

If you permit, I will go now.

اگَربیایَد بِشُما خبَر میدهَم

If he comes, I will tell you.

اگر هنوز نرفته باشدباو حرف میزَنَم

If he has not yet gone, I will speak to him.

When the protasis refers to an action completed before the action of the apodosis, the *Past Tense* may be used.

اگر آمَد بِشُما خَبَر میدِهَم   If he comes, I will tell you.

(*b*) *Impossible*. Both verbs are in the *Imperfect* or *Pluperfect* (cf. para. 76 for this use of the Imperfect).

اگَر زودترمیرَفتید اورا میدیدید   If you had gone sooner, you would have seen him.

اگر دانِسته بودم هَرگِز قَبُول نمیکردم   If I had known, I would never have agreed.

Conditional sentences may also be formed by using the Subjunctive or Imperative without an introductory conjunction, the main verb being in the Indicative.

راستش را بِخواهی دیروز شهر نَرَفتم   (If) you want the truth of it, I did not go to town yesterday.

آن کتاب را بمن بده دیگر چیزی آزت نخواهم خواست   Give me that book (i.e. if you give me that book), I shall not ask anything else from you.

In addition to the concessive conjunctions referred to in paras. 81, 82, 84, اَگَرچه 'although' is commonly used. The tense of the subordinate verb is *Indicative* or *Subjunctive* according to the degree of reality of the condition. The main clause is generally introduced by some such conjunction as بازهَم, وَلی, آمّا etc., or by هَنوز with a negative verb.

اگرچه عجله داشت اَمّا دررا با دقّت قُفل کرد   Although he was in a hurry, (but) he locked the door carefully.

اگرچه اینجا یکسال کارکردم هَنوز رئیس را ملاقات نکرده آم   Although I have worked here for a year, (yet) I have not met the manager.

86. Use of the Infinitive

In its capacity as a verbal noun, the *Infinitive* may be used after verbs of beginning, etc., where the reference is to a general action without an expressed object. The Infinitive is governed by the preposition به.

شُروع کرد بکار کردن   He began to work.

but

شُروع کرد دَر را رَنگ کند   He began to paint the door.

F

87. Logical and Grammatical Subjects

Frequently a complex sentence may open with a logical subject which in fact turns out not to be the same as the grammatical subject of the main verb. A simple example has already been given in Lesson VI (para. 40(ii)). Others are given here.

سَربازانیکه در قَلعـه بودند وَسایلِ
نِجات بَرای آنها نبود

There was no means of escape for the soldiers who were in the fort (lit. the soldiers who were in the fort, there was no means of escape for them).

حَسَن چون تکِ وتَنـها بود دوست
ورَفیقی نبود که اورا کمکِ کند

Since Hasan was alone, there was no friend and companion to help him (lit. Hasan, since he was alone, there was . . .).

منزلیکه آنجا میبینی صاحبش
بَرادَرزادهٔ مَن است

The house that you see there belongs to my nephew (lit. the house that you see there, its owner is my nephew).

این مَردم وقتیکه پاسبانان آمدند
اَوقاتشان تَلخ شد

When the police came, these men became angry (lit. these men, when the police came, their times became bitter).

87a. Intonation Patterns

Conjunctions tend to attract a secondary stress (with high pitch).

Para 84:

harke bašad ‖ meil daram ura bebinam

harkera anja didi ‖ bemanzele man beyavar

har kodam az inhara lazem dari ‖ begir

har ja miravad ‖ ba xošhali esteqbal mikonand

Para. 84a:

cun daxele otaq šod ‖ manzareye qaribi did

karam ra tamam nakardam ‖ ce mixastam te?atr beravam

tɑ cašm kɑr mikard ‖ joz kuh o jangal hic nabud

tɑ injɑ bar gaštid ‖ bešomɑ nešɑn xɑham dɑd

tɑ qabul nakardi ‖ hici naxɑham goft

bɑhuštarid tɑ ‖ yakconin kɑr bekonid

behtar ast injɑ bemɑnim ‖ tɑ dar in havɑ birun rɑvim

rezɑ zarangtar ast tɑ ‖ mohammad

agar ejɑze bedehid ‖ hɑlɑ miravam

agar hanuz narafte bɑšad ‖ beʔu harf mizanam

agar zudtar miraftid ‖ urɑ mididid

rastešra bexɑhi ‖ diruz šahr naraftam

ɑn ketɑbrɑ beman bedeh ‖ digar cizi azat naxɑham xɑst

agarce ajɑle dašt ‖ ammɑ darrɑ bɑ deqqat qofl kard

Para. 86:

šoruʔ kard bekɑr kardan

Para. 87:

sarbɑzɑnike dar qalʔe budand ‖ vasɑyele nejɑt barɑye ɑnhɑ nabud

hasan cun tak o tanhɑ bud ‖ dust o rafiqi nabud ke urɑ ‖ komak
konad

manzelike ɑnjɑ mibini ‖ sɑhebɑš baradarzɑdeye man ast

EXERCISES

A. Translate into English:

عید نوروز

جَمشید یکی از پادشاهان قَدیم داستانهای ایران بوده آست. گویند
پارچه بافتن ولِباس دوختن وجَوکاشتن و خانه ساختن از سَنگَ وگَچ
وگِل را جمشید بمردم یاد داده است. روزی که جمشید برتخت شاهی
نِشَست مَردُم همه خوشحالی کردند، وآن روزرا نَوروز یَعنی روز نَو
اِسم گُذاشتند، و ایرانیان تاکنون این روزرا عید میگیرند. نوروز برای
همهٔ ایرانیان وبِخُصوص برای کودکان بهترین روز سال است. دراین
روز همه لباس نَو میپوشند، بِدیدن هم میروَند، شادی میکنند، و
بِزُرگتران بکودکان عیدی میدهند، یا برای آنان اسباب بازی میخَرَند.

B. Translate into Persian:

The Sasanid empire was still apparently at (in) the zenith of its power when it suddenly succumbed beneath the attack of the Arabs, who, under the influence of their new religion of Islam, poured out of the limits of Arabia during the first half of the seventh century A.D. Within a short time Persia's cultural life became submerged under a surface of Arabic religion, language and administration, even though in fact Persian ideas continually exercised (showed) much influence in the progress of Arabic and Islamic culture. For (In the space of) two centuries the whole of Persia was under the rule of Arabian caliphs, whose capital was first in Arabia, next in Syria, and finally in Iraq; during this time Islam, with its simple, popular ideas, came near to obliterating the old Zoroastrian faith.

VOCABULARY

Jamshid	جَمشید	wheat	گَندُم
story	داستان	barley	جَو
cloth	پارچه	plant	کاشتَن (کار)
weave	بافتَن	plaster	گَچ
sew	دوختَن (دوز)	mud	گِل

sit	نِشَستَن (نِشین)	seventh (see para. 88)	هَفتُم
New Year's Day	نَوروز	A.D.	میلادی
name (v.)	اِسم گُذاشتَن	pour	ریختَن (ریز)
especially	بِخُصوص	pour out	بیرون ریختَن
child	کودَکْ	within, in the space of	دَر ظَرفِ
wear (clothes)	پوشیدَن	surface	سَطح
happiness	شادی	language	زَبان
New Year gift	عَیدی	Arabic	عَرَبی
toy	آسباب بازی	be submerged	غَرق شُدَن
cause, article (pl. آسباب)	سَبَب	in fact	دَر واقِع
play	بازی	continually	دائماً
apparently	ظاهِراً	progress	تَرَقّی
zenith	آوج	Islamic	اِسلامی
power	قُدرَت	caliph (pl. خُلَفا)	خَلیفه
suddenly	ناگاه	next (adv.)	سِپَس
attack	حَمله	finally	آخِر
succumb	مَغلوب گَشتَن	simple	ساده
Arabs	عَرَب	popular	عَوام پَسَند
Islam	اِسلام	idea (pl. عَقایِد)	عَقیده
limit (pl. حُدود)	حَدّ	come near to	نَزدیکْ شُدَن
Arabia	عَرَبِستان	obliterate	مَحو کَردَن
half (n.)	نیمه		

LESSON XIII

Numerals. Time. Age. Dates

88. Cardinal Numbers

(a) The Cardinal Numbers are as follows:

(see para. 28)	یَكْ one.	چِهِل forty.
(see para. 24)	دُو two.	پَنْجاه fifty.
	سِه three.	شَصت sixty.
	چَهار four.	هَفتاد seventy.
	پَنْج five.	هَشتاد eighty.
	شِش six.	نَوَد ninety.
	هَفت seven.	صَد hundred.
	هَشت eight.	یَكْ صَد one hundred.
	نُه nine.	دَویست two hundred.
	دَه ten.	سیصَد three hundred.
	یازدَه eleven.	چَهارصَد four hundred.
	دَوازدَه twelve.	پانصَد five hundred.
	سیزدَه thirteen.	شِشصَد six hundred.
	چَهاردَه fourteen	هَفتصَد seven hundred.
	پانزدَه fifteen.	هَشتصَد eight hundred.
	شانزدَه sixteen.	نُهصَد nine hundred.
	هِفدَه seventeen.	هَزار thousand.
	هیجدَه eighteen.	یَكْ هَزار one thousand, etc.
	نوزدَه nineteen.	کُرُور five hundred thousand.
	بیست twenty.	میلیون million.
	سی thirty.	

(*b*) Compound numerals are formed by linking the parts with the conjunction و, (usually pronounced '*o*'), the largest numeral coming first.

بیست و یکۢ twenty-one.

هَزار و نُهصَد وپَنجاه ونُه 1959.

سی و هَفت هَزار و دَویست و هَشتاد و هَشت 37,288.

(*c*) The Cardinal Numbers normally serve as adjectives, and in conformity with the rule regarding adjectives of quantity and number (see para. 45) precede the noun they qualify, which follows in the singular.

سه مَرد three men.

دَه کِتاب ten books.

The round numbers may also be used in the plural, the following noun however still being in the singular.

دَهها سیب tens (= English dozens) of apples.

صَدها کِتاب hundreds of books.

هَزارها دَرَخت thousands of trees.

هَزاران بَچّه thousands of children.

They may also be used in this way as nouns.

هَزاران آمَدند thousands came.

یَکۢ may be used as a noun with the addition of the indefinite suffix ی . . .

یکی گفت someone said.

Frequently a 'numerator' word is inserted between the numeral and its noun, with some such meaning as 'unit', 'person', etc. This does not add anything to the meaning, and is disappearing in the written language, though in colloquial Persian a few of the very long list of numerators are still commonly heard. The numerator stands as though it were an integral part of the numeral itself, and does not require *ezafe*, nor affect the singular form of the noun. The most usual are, for persons, نَفَر 'person', and تَن 'body'; and for things, تا 'fold' (except in the case of یَک, which takes دانه 'grain').

سه نَفَر پاسبان   three policemen.

صَد تا شُتُر   a hundred camels.

The same construction is used with words that give some definition (size, weight, etc.) to the numeral, as well as with words expressing quantity or type in a more general way.

چهار کیلو گوشت   four kilos of meat.

دو لیوان آب   two glasses of water.

یک دَست لِباس   one suit (lit. hand) of clothes.

سه جُفت کَفش   three pairs of shoes.

شِش نَوع میوه   six kinds of fruit.

In some of these cases the normal *ezafe* construction is also possible, in which case the container or measure becomes the main noun, qualified by the thing contained or measured, e.g.

یَک لیوانْ آب   a glassful (quantity) of water.

but   یک لیوانِ آب   a glass for water, a drinking-glass.

89. The Figures

The figures are those from which the European figures are derived, and still bear some resemblance to them.

۱ ۲ ۳ ٤ ٥ ٥ ٦ ٦ ۷ ۸ ۹ ۰

1 2   3   4   5   6   7 8 9 0

These are written from left to right as in English.

۷۵   75.

۲٤۳   243.

۱۰٦   106.

The letters of the alphabet are also used as numeral figures, mainly nowadays in the pagination of the introductory parts of books, the numbering of paragraphs, etc. (much as in English we use the small Roman numerals i, ii, etc.). Their values are as follows:

ا	ب	ج	د	ه	و	ز	ح	ط	ی	ك	ل	م	ن	س	ع	ف
1	2	3	4	5	6	7	8	9	10	20	30	40	50	60	70	80

ص	ق	ر	ش	ت	ث	خ	ذ	ض	ظ	غ
90	100	200	300	400	500	600	700	800	900	1,000

75. عه

243. رمج

106. قو

For mnemonic purposes the letters as arranged above are grouped into threes and fours as under, forming imaginary words:

أَبْجَد (abjad)   هَوَّز (havvez)   حُطّى (hotti)

كَلَمَن (kaleman)   سَعْفَص (sa?fas)   قَرِشَت (qarešat)

ثَخَّذ (saxxaz)   ضَظِّغ (zazzeq)

From these are taken the word for *alphabet* أَبْجَد, and the distinguishing names of the two letters *he* (see paras. 8, 24).

90. Ordinal Numbers

The ordinal numbers are for the most part formed by adding the suffix مُ . . . to the cardinal numeral.

پَنْجُم   fifth.

بِیسْتُم   twentieth.

چِهِل ویکُم   forty-first.

دَوِیست و هَفْتاد و هَشْتُم   two hundred and seventy-eighth.

'First' is generally used in the Arabic form أَوَّل (though not in compound numbers—see 'forty-first' above). 'Two' and 'three' are slightly modified in the ordinal form:

(pron. *doyom*) دُوُّم، دُوُیُم second.

سِوُّم، سِیُم third.

The ordinals are employed as normal adjectives, following the noun qualified in the *ezafe* construction.

مَردِ سِوُّم the third man.

صَفِّ چَهاردَهُم the fourteenth row.

A 'superlative' form of the ordinal numerals, with the additional suffix یِن . . . , is used to indicate position in a series. As with the superlative adjectives (see para. 38), the numeral precedes the noun without *ezafe*.

بیست وسِوُّمیْن روزِماه the twenty-third day of the month.

چَهارصَد وبیست وهَفتُمیْن شُمارهٔ روزنامه the 427th issue of the newspaper.

اَوَّل may also take this suffix, and its opposite, آخِرین 'last', should also be noticed.

اَوَّلیْن روزِ سال the first day of the year.

آخِرین مَنزِلِ خیابان the last house in the street.

91. Fractions

Ordinal numbers are increasingly being used to represent the fractions.

دو سِوُّم two-thirds.

چهار نُهُم four-ninths.

Alternatively, the Arabic forms of the fractions are commonly used:

نِصف half.   رُبع quarter.

ثُلَث third.   خُمس fifth.

سُدس sixth.   عُشر tenth.

سُبع seventh.   دُو ثُلث two-thirds.

ثُمن eighth.   چهار تُسع four-ninths.

تُسع ninth.

Another construction often found places the denominator first, followed by the numerator, both in the cardinal form. This is nowadays only used when the numerator is يك.

سه يكك   one-third (lit. (of) three, one).

A modification of this construction is used to express percentages.

صَدى پانزدَه   fifteen per cent. (lit. (of) a hundred, fifteen).

The Persian word for 'half', نيم, is used in combination with other numerals. It normally follows the noun governed, as do the other fractions, when combined with whole numbers.

سه مِتر و نيم $3\frac{1}{2}$ metres.

دو ساعَت و سه رَبع $2\frac{3}{4}$ hours.

but   سه رُبعْ ساعَت   three-quarters of an hour.

92. Other Expressions of Number

يَكى يَكى   one by one.

دوتا دوتا   two by two, etc.

دو سه   two or three, etc.

هَردو   both.

هرسه   all three, etc.

دو بار (دَفعه، مَرتَبه)   twice, etc. (lit. two times).

دو مَرتَبه is also used in the sense of 'again'. Cf. also

دو باره   again.

93. Arithmetical Expressions

Addition (جَمع):

هَفت و چَهار میشَوَد یازدَه (تا)   seven and four make eleven.

Subtraction (تَفریق):

سه اَز نُه میشَوَد (میمانَد) شِش (تا)   three from nine make six.

Multiplication (ضرَب):

پَنج هَفت تا میشَوَد سی و پَنج (تا)   five times seven is thirty-five.

Division (تَقسیم):

دَه تَقسیم بَردو میشَوَد پَنج (تا)   two into ten is five.

94. Time

ساعتْ چَند است؟   What is the time? (lit. the hour how much is it?).

ساعتِ چهار است   It is four o'clock (lit. the hour of four).

ساعتِ چَهار ونیم است   It is half *past* four (lit. the hour of four and a half).

ساعتِ چهار وپنج دَقیقه است   It is five minutes *past* four (lit. the hour of four and five minutes).

ساعتِ چهارْ رُبع کَم است   It is a quarter *to* four (lit. the hour of four, a quarter less).

ساعتِ چَهارْ دَه دَقیقه کَم است   It is ten *to* four (lit. the hour of four, ten minutes less).

95. Age

چَند سال دارید؟   How old are you? (lit. how many years have you?).

بیست سال دارَم   I am twenty years old (lit. I have twenty years).

Alternative expressions are to be found for all the examples in paras. 93–95, but those given are the commonest and simplest.

96. Dates

(*a*) The days of the week are as follows:

شَنبه	Saturday.
یَکشَنبه	Sunday.
دوشَنبه	Monday.
سه شَنبه	Tuesday.
چَهارشَنبه	Wednesday.
پَنجشَنبه	Thursday.
جُمعه	Friday (the day of rest, lit. of gathering).

The name of the day may precede the time of day without *ezafe*, or follow it with *ezafe*.

یَکشَنبه صُبح، صُبحِ یَکشَنبه	Sunday morning.
چَهارشَنبه ظُهر، ظُهرِ چَهارشَنبه	Wednesday noon.
پَنجشَنبه عَصر، عَصرِ پَنجشَنبه	Thursday afternoon.

The early part of the afternoon may be expressed by the phrase
بَعد از ظُهر.

Great care must however be taken over the use of the word شَب 'evening', since according to the *traditional* reckoning (no longer used officially, but common in everyday speech) the day begins at sunset, and the evening is therefore the first part of what we would regard as the *following* day (cf. English 'eve').

شَبِ جُمعه   therefore means: *Thursday* evening.

But the modern usage is differentiated by using the qualifying word in the preceding position.

پَنجشَنبه شَب	Thursday evening.
جُمعه شَب، شَبِ شَنبه	Friday evening.

(*b*) Although both the Moslem (lunar—قَمَری) and the Christian calendars are known in Persia, the generally accepted one is the old Persian reckoning modified to accord with the Moslem (هِجری)

era, and officially introduced in 1924. The year is a solar (شَمسی) one, reckoned from A.D. 622 (سال ۱ هِجری شَمسی =), and begins on approximately 21 March of each Christian year. The year 1339 began on 21 March 1960.

The Persian months are as follows (with approximate equivalents):

فَروَرْدین   31 days (21 Mar.–20 Apr.).

أُردیبِهِشت   31 days (21 Apr.–21 May).

خُرداد   31 days (22 May–21 June).

تیر   31 days (22 June–22 July).

مُرداد   31 days (23 July–22 Aug.).

شَهریوَر   31 days (23 Aug.–22 Sept.).

مِهر   30 days (23 Sept.–22 Oct.).

آبان   30 days (23 Oct.–21 Nov.).

آذَر   30 days (22 Nov.–21 Dec.).

دَی   30 days (22 Dec.–20 Jan.).

بَهمَن   30 days (21 Jan.–19 Feb.).

إسفَند   29 days (20 Feb.–20 Mar.).

   (30 days in a leap-year).

Leap years (سال کَبیسه) occur every four years (except that every eighth leap year comes after an interval of five years—that is to say, a cycle of eight leap years takes 33 years instead of 32). Since the Persian leap years do not coincide with those of the Christian reckoning, there is periodically a shift of one day in the equivalent dates given above. Thus the Persian year *immediately following* the Persian leap year starts on 22 March (all subsequent dates in the same year being correspondingly affected), and at present this is corrected in the following year (back to 21 March) by the incidence of the Christian leap year.

Thus 1337 (leap year) began on 21 March 1958; 1338 began on 22 March 1959; 1339 began on 21 March 1960 (leap year).

The day of the month is expressed by the ordinal number, followed by the name of the month with *ezafe*. The name of the month may stand alone, or take the word ماه 'month' either preceding with *ezafe* or following without. The year is expressed by the word سال 'year' followed by the number with *ezafe*.

Thursday, 28th Azar, 1336 A.H.S. (روز) پَنجشَنبه، بیست وهَشتُمِ

آذَر (آذَرماه، ماه آذَر)، سال هَزَارو

سیصَدوسی وشِشِ هِجری شَمسی

= پَنجشَنبه، ۲۸ آذَر ۱۳۳۶ هـ.ش.

= ۳٦/۹/۲۸

96a. Intonation Patterns

Para. 93:

haft o cahar ‖ misavad yazdah tɑ

Para. 94:

saʔat cand ast

saʔate cahar o nim ast

Para. 95:

cand sɑl dɑrid

bist sɑl dɑram

EXERCISES

A. Translate into English:

روزِ سه شَنبه ۱٤ مرداد ۱۳۳۷ عِمارت جدید و مُجَلَّل فُرودگاهِ

مِهرآباد بِدست مبارکِ آعلَیحضرتَهُمایون شاهَنشاهی گُشایش یافت.

بنای این عِمارت، که در نوعِ خود در سراسَرِ جهان کَم نظیر است،

از لِحاظِ حِفظِ حَیثیاتِ کشور در اَنظارِ خارجیان، که مُرتَّباً آز این

فرودگاه مسافرت میکنُنَند، ورَفعِ احتیاجاتِ روز، اِقدامِ بسیار مُهِمّ و مُفیدَ بشمار میرَوَد. وجودِ یَکِ فرودگاهِ مُجهَّزبَ ستگاه‌های کامِلِ فَنّی مُتَناسب باترقی بُزُرگِ هَواپِیمائیِ اِمروز مَوجب میشَوَد که شِرکتهایِ بزرگِ هواپیمائیِ جهان سَعی کنند چنین فرودگاهی را در مسیرِ خطوطِ پَروازیِ خود قرار دهند، وطبیعی است که ازاین لحاظ آوَلاً منافعِ زیادی عایدِ مملکت میشَوَد، وثانیًا در شِناسائیِ تَمدُّنِ کشور بمردمِ جهان بطورِ شایسته‌ای مؤثّر اُفتد.

B. Translate into Persian:

Independent dynasties began to appear in Iran during the second and third centuries A.H. Among the most famous of those were the Samanids in Khorasan and Transoxania and the Buyids in central and south Persia. Famous Persian poets like Rudaki and Ferdousi made their name during this period. Towards the end (In the last parts) of the fourth century A.H. the powerful Turkish monarch, Mahmud of Ghazne, ruled in the east, and in the middle (parts) of the fifth century the whole country was occupied by the Seljuqs from central Asia. For (In) the next five-hundred-year period the same sequence of events is repeated; the appearance of small independent dynasties is interrupted by (means of) catastrophic invasions, among which must be mentioned that of the Mongols in the seventh century and of Tamerlane in the eighth century. In spite of this, it was during this time that Persia's loftiest achievements in literature and fine arts were manifested. But it was only in the beginning of the tenth century A.H. that a true Persian dynasty ruled once again over (on) the whole country.

VOCABULARY

Tuesday	سه شَنبه	Mehrabad	مِهرآباد
Mordad (name of month)	مُرداد	blessed	مُبارَک
new	جَدید	majesty[1]	اَعلیَحَضرَت
splendid	مُجَلَّل	imperial	شاهَنشاهی
airport	فُرودگاه	august	هُمایون

[1] Pronounced aʾlɑhazrat (see para. 57, note [1]).

be open	گُشایَش یا فتَن	flying (adj.)	پَروازی
construction	بَنا	establish	قِرار دادَن
kind	نَوع	natural	طَبیعی
exceptional	کَم نَظیر	firstly	اَوَّلاً
aspect	لِحاظ	profit (pl. مَنافِع)	مَنفَعَت
preservation	حِفظ	accruing	عایِد
qualities	حَیثیات	secondly	ثانیاً
sight (pl. آنظار)	نَظَر	civilization	تَمَدُّن
foreign(er)	خارِجی	making known (trans. noun)	شِناسائی
regularly	مُرَتَّباً	worthy	شایِسته
travel	مُسافَرَت کَردَن	be effective	مُؤَثِّر اُفتادَن
removal	رَفع	independent	مُستَقِلّ
needs	اِحتیاجات	begin	شُروع کَردَن
step, advance	اِقدام	A.H.	هِجری
useful	مُفید	appear	ظُهور یافتَن
important	مُهِمّ	among	مابَین
be reckoned	بِشُمار رَفتَن	second	دُوُّم
existence	وُجود	third	سِوُّم
equipped	مُجَهَّز	Samanids	آل سامان
apparatus	دَستگاه	Khorasan	خُراسان
complete	کامِل	Transoxania [see para. 108(a)]	ماوَرایَ النَّهر
technical	فَنّی	Buyids	آل بویه
appropriate	مُتَناسِب	poet (pl. شُعَرا)	شاعِر
aeronautical	هَواپیَیمائی	like	مِثلِ
cause	مَوجِب	Rudaki	رودَکی
company	شِرکَت	Ferdousi	فِردَوسی
course, route	مَسیر		

make one's name	شُهرَت یافتَن	be repeated	تِکرار شُدَن
fourth	چَهارُم	appearance	ظُهور
Turkish	تُرکی	be interrupted	قَطع شُدَن
powerful	نیرومَند	by means of	تَوَسُّط
monarch	سُلطان	catastrophic	مَصیبَت آوَر
Mahmud	مَحمود	mention	ذِکر کَردَن
Ghazne	غَزنه	Mongols, Moguls	مُغَول
east	شَرق	Tamerlane	تیمور لَنگ
middle parts	آواسِط	eighth	هَشتُم
fifth	پَنجُم	in spite of	با وُجودِ
occupy	اِشغال کَردَن	lofty	عالی
Seljuq	سلجوق	achievement	شاهکار
five-hundred-year (adj.)	پانصَدساله	literature	آدَبیات
next	بَعد	fine arts	صَنایِعِ ظَریفه
sequence	رِشته	be manifested	بُروز شُدَن
event (pl. حَوادِث)	حادِثه	tenth	دَهُم

LESSON XIV

Persian Word Formation

97. Derivation of Words

The two lessons that follow are intended as a guide to the accumulation and expansion of vocabulary. Most of the words described may be found in a good dictionary, but ready recognition of some of the commoner compound types will assist the student to free himself from dependence on dictionaries and vocabularies.

In this chapter the Persian methods of forming words will be described, the Arabic methods being discussed in Lesson XV. Persian offers three main methods: prefixes (comparatively rare), suffixes, and juxtaposition. In all cases a basic word is qualified or defined by whatever is added.

98. Prefixes

The two most significant prefixes are نا 'un-' and هَم 'co-'.

پاك	clean.	ناپاك	unclean, dirty.
[دان]	knowing	نادان	unknowing, ignorant.
	(Pres. stem of دانِستن).		
خُوش	good, well.	ناخُوش	unwell, ill.
وَطَن	country.	هَموَطَن	compatriot.
راه	road.	هَمراه	together, companion.
كار	work.	هَمكار	colleague.

99. Suffixes

Certain suffixes are used very freely, others are limited to certain dictionary words. In general each is confined to the formation of either nouns or adjectives, but it must be remembered that the line between these two parts of speech is not very sharply drawn. All these suffixes, being an integral part of the word, take the final stress.

(a) ی . . . (i) affixed to adjectives and certain types of noun and adverb, to form abstract nouns.

خوب	good.	خوبی	goodness.
بُزُرگ	large.	بُزُرگی	largeness.
مَرد	man.	مَردی	manliness.
تَنها	alone.	تَنهائی	loneliness.
نَجّار	carpenter.	نَجّاری	carpentry.

When this ی . . . is suffixed to a word of Persian origin ending in ه . . . , the *he* is replaced by a *gaf*.

بَچه	child.	بَچگی	childhood.

(ii) affixed to nouns to form relative adjectives.

ایران	Iran.	ایرانی	Iranian.

تِهران	Tehran.	تِهرانی	Tehrani.
آب	water.	آبی	(water-coloured), blue.
دِهات	villages, countryside.	دهاتی	villager, peasant.
اینجا	here.	اینجائی	from these parts.

When suffixed to a word ending in ه . . ., this suffix is usually written as a separate particle, using the initial *alef* (contrast with (*a*) (i) above).

کِناره	coast.	کِنارهای	coastal.

Both these suffixes may be employed very freely, and can often be added to prepositional phrases, etc., e.g.

بی وَفائی	disloyalty (lit. without-loyalty-ness) (see para. 100 (*c*)).

(*b*) ه . . . (i) added to nouns to modify their meaning, often in the sense of a group.

دَست	hand.	دَسته	handle, handful.
گوش	ear.	گوشه	corner.
چَشم	eye.	چشمه	spring (water).
پَنج	five.	پَنجه	hand (i.e. five fingers).
هَفت	seven.	هَفته	week (i.e. seven days).

(ii) added to a group consisting of a numeral, a pronominal adjective or similar word, and a noun to form an adjective or noun.

دَه سال	ten years.	دَه ساله	ten years old.
دو چَرخ	two wheels.	دو چَرخه	bicycle.
چَهار مُتور	four engines.	چَهار مُتوره	four-engined (plane, etc.).
چه کار	what work?	چِکاره	of what occupation?
هَمه کار all work. هیچ کار no work.		همه کاره و هیچکاره	Jack of all trades.

(c) انه . . . added to nouns and adjectives applicable to persons to form adjectives applicable to actions or objects.

عاقِل	intelligent.	کار عاقِلانه	an intelligent action.
أُستاد	master.	أُستادانه	masterly.
شاعِر	poet.	شاعِرانه	poetical.
بَچه	child.	بَچِگانه	childish.

This ending is often exclusively adverbial in use:

خوشبختانه   luckily.

مُتَأسّفانه   unfortunately, regrettably.

(d) The next six suffixes may only be used with Persian verbal stems.

ش . . . added to the Present Stem to form a Verbal Noun.

| خواستن | wish, Pres. Stem. خواه : | خواهِش | wish, request (noun). |
| کوشیدن | try, Pres. Stem. کوش : | کوشِش | effort. |

(e) نده . . . added to the Present Stem to form the Agent; also used as a descriptive adjective.

نَمودن	show, Pres. Stem. نَما :	نَمایَنده	representative.
نَوِشتن	write, Pres. Stem. نَویس :	نَویسَنده	writer.
آمدن	come, Pres. Stem. آ :	آیَنده	coming, future.

(f) ان . . . added to the Present Stem to form an adjective describing a temporary condition.

| سوختن | burn, Pres. Stem. سوز : | سوزان | burning. |
| لَرزیدن | tremble, Pres. Stem. لَرز : | لَرزان | trembling. |

(g) ا . . . added to the Present Stem to form an adjective describing a permanent quality.

| دانِستن | know, Pres. Stem. دان : | دانا | knowing, wise. |
| تَوانِستن | be able, Pres. Stem. توان : | تَوانا | powerful. |

(h) ـَنی . . . added to the Past Stem to form an adjective (or noun) expressing necessary, desirable or future action.

رَفتَن	go.	رَفتَنی	about to go.
خریدن	buy.	خَریدَنی	worth buying.
دیدن	see.	دیدَنی	worth seeing.
گُفتَن	say.	گُفتَنی	that has to be said.

(i) ار . . . added to the Past Stem to form an abstract noun (sometimes also an adjective or an agent [1]).

رَفتَن	go.	رَفتار	way of going, conduct.
گِرِفتَن	take.	گِرِفتار	occupied, victim.
خریدن	buy.	خریدار	customer.

The remaining suffixes are added to nouns to form adjectives or nouns.

(j) ـگَر. . . , گار . . . , کار . . . , چی . . . , بان . . . added to nouns (occasionally verbal stems) to describe occupations.

کار	work.	کارگَر	worker.
آموز Pres. Stem. , آموختَن teach	آموزگار	teacher.
خِدمَت	service.	خِدمَتکار	servant, employee.
طَیّاره	aeroplane.	طَیّاره چی	pilot (somewhat colloquial).
باغ	garden.	باغبان	gardener.

(k) دان . . . added to nouns to describe containers, etc.

قَلَم	pen.	قَلَمدان	pen-case.
نَمَک	salt.	نَمَکدان	salt-cellar.

(l) ـِستان . . . added to nouns to form nouns of place.

گُل	rose.	گُلِستان	rose-garden.
اَفغان	Afghan.	اَفغانِستان	Afghanistan.
بیمار	sick.	بیمارِستان	hospital.

---

[1] This was actually the original use.

(m) چه . . . , کک . . . added to nouns to form diminutives, sometimes with modification of meaning.

دُختَر	girl.	دُختَرَکک	little girl.
کِتاب	book.	کِتابچه	note-book.
صورَت	face.	صورَتَکک	mask.
چَشم	eye.	چَشمَکک	wink.

(n) وار . . . , وَر . . . , مَند . . . added to nouns to indicate the possession of a quality.

ثَروَت	wealth.	ثَروَتمَند	rich.
کار	work.	کارمَند	employee, member.
سُخَن	word.	سُخَنوَر	poet.
أُمید	hope.	أُمیدوار	hopeful.

(o) گین . . . , ناکک . . . added to nouns (generally abstract) to express possession of an unpleasant quality.

| خَطَر | danger. | خَطَرناکک | dangerous. |
| غَم | sorrow. | غَمگین | sorrowful. |

(p) ین . . . added to nouns (generally materials) to form adjectives.

آهَن	iron (noun).	آهَنین	iron (adj.).
سیم	silver.	سیمین	silver.
رَنگک	colour.	رَنگین	coloured.
سَنگک	stone.	سَنگین	heavy.

100. Juxtaposition

The bulk of the words formed in this category consist of a basic word (often of a general character), together with a qualifying word that normally precedes it.

(a) Noun, adjective, verbal stem qualifying or defining a noun of place, etc.

خانه house.   مَریضخانه (sick-house)—hospital.

کارخانه (work-house)—factory.

گاه place.   خوابگاه (sleep-place)—bedroom.

ایستگاه (stopping-place)—station.

نامه letter.   روزنامه (day-letter)—newspaper.

شِناسنامه (knowing-letter)—identity card.

(b) Noun or adjective qualifying a noun to form an adjective.

خوشبو sweet-smelling.

گُلرَنگ rose-coloured.

سَنگدِل stony-hearted.

فارسی زَبان Persian-speaking (lit. -tongued).

چهارپا four-footed, quadruped.

حَسَن نام Hasan by name.

گُم نام unknown (lit. lost-name).

Sometimes two or more nouns may be used.

خوش قَد و بالا of good figure and stature, shapely.

(c) Preposition governing a noun (see para. 61).

باوَفا faithful.

بی اِنصاف unjust.

(d) Noun, adjective, etc., defining a verbal Present Stem.

قالی فُروش carpet-seller.

ساعَت ساز watch-maker.

دُروغگو (lie-teller), untruthful.

تُند نَویس (quick-writer), stenographer.

خُشککُن (dry-making), blotting-paper.

حَق شِناس (due-recognizing), grateful.

دوربین (far-seeing), telescope, camera.

This is an extremely common and flexible method of forming words, and may be used extensively outside the strict limits of 'dictionary' words, as the following examples, taken from modern Persian writers, illustrate:

مال ِ مَردُم خوُر
profiteer (lit. money-of-people-eater).

شرح حال ِ اَشخاصِ گُمنام نویس [1]
biographer of unknown persons (lit. story-of-life-of-unknown-persons-writer).

مُوافَقَتهای شوم و ایران بَرباد دِه [1]
tragic treaties that destroy Persia (lit. tragic and Persia-to-the-wind-giving treaties).

Sometimes the verbal element is of a general character, serving almost as a suffix to the 'qualifying' word. Characteristic verbal stems of this type include:

اَنگیختَن) اَنگیز to stir up)   آمیختَن) آمیز to mix).

آوَردَن) آوَر to bring)   پَذیرُفتَن) پَذیر to receive).

سِحر آمیز (magic-mixing), magical, enchanting.

شور آنگیز (excitement-arousing), exciting.

اِمکان پَذیر (possibility-receiving), possible.

وَحشَت آوَر (alarm-bringing), alarming.

(e) Noun, adjective, etc., defining a verbal Past Stem or Participle.

جَهان دیده (world-seen), experienced.

شاهزاده (king-born), prince.

خواب آلود(ه) (sleep-stained), sleepy.

---

[1] I am indebted for these examples to Gilbert Lazard's *Grammaire du Persan Contemporain*.

(f) In a few cases, mainly verbal stems, the two parts are complementary rather than one qualifying the other.

جُسْتُجو   search.

گَفْتُگو   conversation.

آمَد و رَفت   coming and going, traffic.

خَرید و فُروش   buying and selling, trade.

(g) Many pairs of words linked by the ordinary *ezafe* construction have acquired the status of compound nouns, and may even take the plural ending after the qualifying word.

سیبِ زَمینی   potato (ground-apple)   سیبِ زَمینیها potatoes.

گُلِ سُرخ   rose (red flower)   گُلِ سُرخها roses.

شَرحِ حال   biography.

سوءِ تَفَاهُم   misunderstanding.

سوءِ ظَنّ   distrust.

In a few cases the *ezafe* is omitted.

دُختَرْ عَمو   (daughter [of] uncle), cousin.

صاحِبْ خانه   (owner [of] house), landlord, host.

صاحِبْدِل   (owner [of] heart), romantic, sentimental.

101. Doubly Compound Words

Two or more of these methods may be combined.

قالی فروشی (قالی + فروش + ی)   carpet-selling.

آهَنگَری (آهَن + گَر + ی)   iron-working.

باوَرنکردنی (باوَر + نَه + کَرد + نی)   unbelievable.

شِکَست ناپَذیر (شِکَست + نا + پَذیر)   invincible.

مَردانگی (مَرد + انه + ی)   manliness.

دیوانه وار (دیو + انه + وار)   like a madman.

The above lists of suffixes and types of compound word are not intended to be exhaustive, but include only those most commonly encountered. The student will be able to accumulate additional examples for himself.

102. Derived Verbs

A considerable number of simple verbs may be formed from nouns by the addition of ‮یدَن‬ . . . to form the *Infinitive*.

‮دُزد‬	thief.	‮دُزدیدن‬	steal.
‮نام‬	name.	‮نامیدن‬	name (verb).

This form is also used with nouns of Arabic and other foreign origin.

‮طَلَب‬	request (noun).	‮طَلَبیدن‬	request (verb).
		(‮طَلَب کردن‬ also)	
‮فَهم‬	understanding.	‮فَهمیدن‬	understand.

Causative verbs may be formed by adding ‮ان‬ . . . to the Present Stem of the Simple verb to form the new *Present Stem*. The corresponding *Infinitive* is formed regularly by adding ‮یدَن‬ . . . or ‮دَن‬ . . ..

‮رَسیدن‬	arrive.	‮رَساندن، رَسانیدن‬	cause to arrive, deliver.
‮فَهمیدن‬	understand.	‮فَهماندن‬	make to understand.

In some cases contractions take place.

‮رَفتن‬	go.	‮راندن‬	cause to go, drive
		(for ‮رواندن‬]).	
‮نِشَستن‬	sit.	‮نِشاندن‬	cause to sit, seat
		(for ‮نِشیناندن‬]).	

The *Present Stem* ‮گُذَر‬ 'pass' forms the Causative by inserting ‮ا‬ . . . in the second syllable. The normal form is also used, so that three versions of the verb exist.

‮گُذَراندن (گُذَران‬ stem)   make to pass, spend (time), etc.

‮گُذاشتن‬
‮گُذاردن‬ (‮گُذار‬ stem)   make to pass, leave, put, allow.

EXERCISES

A. Translate into English:

ستارهٔ «تِشتَر» فرِشتهٔ باران بود. هُرمُزد چون از آفرینشِ جهان فراغت
یافت، ستارهٔ تِشتَر را بآبیاریِ جهان گُماشت تا از ابرباران ببارد و زمین را
سیراب کنـد، وکِشوَرهای آریائی را سبز و آباد نمایـد. آهریمن بَدنهـاد،
که دُشمنِ نیکی و آبادی بود، چون خوبیِ جهانِ هُرمزد را دید، خَشمگین
شد. «آپوش» دیو خُشکی را برآن گُماشت تا بادِ گَرم بوَزاند و زمینها را
خشک کنـد. آنگاه ستاره تشتر طلوع کرد و بیاریِ هرمزد برخاست.
نُخُست خود را بصورتِ جوانی پانزده ساله در آورد و مُدَّتِ ده شبان
روز در آسمان پرواز کرد و از ابرها باران بارید. سپَس خود را بصورتِ
گاوِ زَرّین شاخ در آورد و ده شبان روز در آسمان پرواز کرد واز ابرهـا
باران بارید. سوُّم بار خود را بصورت اسب سفید در آورد وده شبان
روز در آسمان پرواز کرد و از ابرها باران بارید. قطراتِ باران هر یکِ
بدُرُشتیِ یکِ پیاله بود. آب بقامتِ یکِ مرد بالا آمد وسراسرِ زمین را
فراگرفت. جانورانِ زیانبَخش همه هلاکِ شُدند و در سوراخهای زمین
فُرو رفتند.

B. Translate into Persian:

The Safavid dynasty was founded by Shah Esma'il, who ascended
(sat on) the royal throne in 907 A.H. He and his successors united Persia
into one empire, and established the Shi'a sect of Islam [as] the national
religion of Persia; by this means they restored the unity of religion and
state that had existed in the days of the Sasanids a thousand years earlier.
The reign of the Safavids achieved its greatest glory in the age of Shah
Abbas I, who was the contemporary of Queen Elizabeth of England, the
Mogul emperor Akbar, and the Ottoman Sultan Soleiman. Isfahan, the
capital, and other cities were adorned with beautiful mosques and palaces,
literature and the fine arts were encouraged, and friendly relations were
created with the great nations of Asia and Europe. The Safavid dynasty
collapsed in the middle of the twelfth century A.H., and after an interval
of anarchy and Afghan invasions, the throne was occupied by Nader
Shah, who, in a short period of glory, expanded the Persian empire
from the Caucasus to the river Indus. After his death the empire once

again broke up, though for thirty years Karim Khan Zand ruled a large part of the country from Shiraz. At (In) the beginning of the thirteenth century A.H., corresponding to the nineteenth century A.D., the Qajar chieftain Aqa Mohammad defeated his rivals, and placed his capital at (in) Tehran.

VOCABULARY

star	ستاره	blow (v. trans.)	وَزانیدَن
Sirius	تِشتَر	then	آنگاه
angel	فِرِشته	rise (star)	طُلوع کَردَن
rain (n.)	باران	help (n.)	یاری
Hormozd	هُرمُزد	rise up	بَر خاستَن
creation	آفَرینِش	first	نُخُست
finish	فِراغَت یافتَن آز	form	صورَت
irrigation	آبیاری	produce	دَر آوَردَن
appoint	گُماشتَن (گُمار)	period, interval	مُدَّت
cloud	آبر	day and night	شَبان روز
rain (v. intr.)	باریدَن	fly (v.)	پَرواز کَردَن
soaked	سیراب	bull, cow	گاو
cultivated	آباد	golden	زَرّین
Ahriman	اَهریمَن	horn	شاخ
bad-natured	بَدنِهاد	horse	اَسب
enemy	دُشمَن	white	سَفید
good	نیک	drop (pl. قَطَرات)	قَطره
angry	خَشمگین	large	دُرُشت
demon	دیو	cup	پیاله
dry	خُشک	height	قامَت
wind	باد	envelop (v.)	فَراگِرِفتَن
hot, warm	گَرم	animal	جانوَر

harmful	زیانبَخش
be destroyed	هَلاک شُدَن
hole	سوراخ
go down	فرُو رفتَن
Safavid	صَفَوی
Shah	شاه
Esma'il	اِسماعیل
throne	تَخت
successor	جانشین
unite	مُتّحِد کَردَن
sect	مَذهَب
Shi'a (adj.)	شیعه ای
restore	قِرارگُذاشتَن
unity	اِتّحاد
state	دَولَت
day (pl. اَیّام)	یَوم
earlier	قَبل
exist	وُجود داشتَن
glory	رَونَق
age	عَصر
achieve	. . . نایِل شُدَن به
Abbas	عَبّاس
contemporary	مُعاصِر
queen	مَلِکه
Elizabeth	اِلیزابِت
England	اِنگِلستان
Akbar	اَکبَر

sultan	سُلطان
Ottoman	عُثمانی
Soleiman	سُلَیمان
Isfahan	اِصفَهان
palace	کاخ
adorn	آرایِش دادَن
encourage	تَشویق کَردَن
friendly	دوستانه
create	اِیجاد نَمودَن
collapse	بِهَم خُوردَن
anarchy	اِغتِشاش
Afghan	آفغان
occupy	تَصَرّف کَردَن
Nader	نادِر
Caucasus	قَفقاز
Indus river	رودِ سِند
Karim Khan Zand	کَریم خان زَند
part	قِسمَت
Shiraz	شیراز
beginning	اِبتِدا
corresponding to	مُطابِق
nineteenth	نوزدَهُم
Qajar	قاجار
Aqa Mohammad	آقا مُحَمَّد
rival (pl. رُقَبا)	رَقیب
place (v.) (گُذار)	گُذاشتَن

LESSON XV

The Arabic Element in Persian

103. The Triliteral Root

Arabic grammar and syntax has not affected the structure of Persian to any great extent. But Arabic influence on Persian vocabulary has been enormous, and though spasmodic efforts have been made in recent years, both officially and by individual writers, to reduce the use of Arabic words, it is unlikely that any marked impression will be made on everyday usage, any more than it has been possible to eliminate Latin from English.

It will be necessary first of all to consider the peculiar method of word construction in Arabic—a method characteristic of all the Semitic languages. In the Indo-European languages (such as English and Persian), words are built up, by means of prefixes, suffixes, phonetic changes, etc., from roots which may at one time have existed in some form as words, but which have only rarely survived as such, and are of little practical value so far as the study of the modern language is concerned.

The Arabic root is exactly the opposite; it is purely theoretical (as will be seen, it consists entirely of consonants), but it is of the greatest grammatical importance. Once the root is isolated, a whole series of words, with fairly well-defined shades of meaning, may be formed from it according to precise 'mathematical' formulae.

The majority of Arabic words are formed from triliteral (three-consonant) roots; a few roots have four consonants, while in some cases only two have survived. To these three (or four) consonants are added vowels and often additional consonants; one of the original consonants may also be doubled. Thus from the basic root *k-t-b*, containing the idea of 'writing', may be derived:

kataba	he wrote.
ya*ktubu*	he is writing.
kitāb	book.
ma*ktab*	office, school.
ma*ktūb*	letter.
*kitāb*at	writing.
kātib, pl. *kuttāb*	writer, clerk.

as well as many other forms. Where one of the consonants is *w* (= *v* in Persian), *y*, or *hamze*, contraction may take place, and the root is not then always readily distinguishable; such contraction however conforms to regular rules, and can generally be recognized without much difficulty, e.g.

bannā   mason, for [*bannāy*], root *b-n-y* (build).

idārat   department, administration, for [*idwārat*], root *d-w-r* (revolve).

Many of the formulae, for instance those making up the conjugation of the verb, are rarely found in Persian, while others are not governed by distinctive rules. The examples discussed in the following paragraphs, however, have sufficient regularity in use to make them helpful in the building of vocabulary. The Arabic origin of a word may often be determined by the fact that it contains one of the eight letters (see para. 31) that occur mainly or exclusively in Arabic words.

104. The Formulae

The Arab and Persian grammarians at an early date adopted the three consonants ل, ع, ف (containing the basic idea of 'doing') as token consonants to describe the various formulae. Thus the word کِتاب is said to be of the form فِعال; مَکتوب of the form مَفعول; and so on. It must be understood that the formulae themselves do not necessarily or even normally have any meaning of their own.

105. Noun Formulae

(a) The Broken Plural

By far the most important group of noun formulae is the Broken Plural. The majority of Arabic plurals are formed, not by the addition of a suffix, but by an internal change in the word (see para. 28), that is, by the use of another formula. There is generally no relationship between the formula used for the singular noun and that used for its plural, nor even consistency in the pairing of singular and plural formulae; while the same formula may be used in one instance for the singular, and in another for the plural.

کِتاب book, pl. کُتُب .

رَجُل man, pl. رِجال .

The correct use of the Arabic Broken Plural must, therefore, be largely a matter of learning vocabulary; however, a few of the more distinctive forms are given below as a guide.

(i) فُعول:

حَدّ	limit	حُدود	
أمر	affair	أُمور	
مَلِكْ	king	مُلوكْ	

(ii) أفعال:

شَخص	person	أشخاص	
صاحِب	owner	أصحاب	
وقت	time	أوقات	

(iii) فُعُل:

كِتاب	book	كُتُب	
طَريق	road	طُرُق	
مَدينه	city	مُدُن	

(iv) فُعَلا (particularly linked with the singular forms فَعيـل and فاعِل):

رَئيس	chief, director	رُؤَسا	
شاعِر	poet	شُعَرا	
وَزير	minister	وُزَرا	

(v) فَعاليل, فَعالِل:

Formulae of this type are particularly common when the singular form consists of four or more letters (excluding the Arabic feminine suffix, see para. 108 (b)). The fourth letter may be: (1) an additional root letter, (2) a grammatical prefix such as م (see (b) and (c) below) or ا, (3) a long vowel.

G

Four-letter singulars use the plural form فَعَالِـل.

(1)

كَوكَب   star   pl. كَوَاكِب (root كـ و كـ ب).

جَوهَر   jewel, ink   pl. جَوَاهِـر (root ج و ه ر).

(2)

مَسجِد   mosque   pl. مَساجِد (root س ج د).

أَكبَر   elder   pl. أَكابِر (root كـ ب ر).

(3) When the fourth letter is a 'long' vowel, a و or ى is added in the plural form.

ساحِل   shore   pl. سَوَاحِل (root س ح ل).

رابِطه   connection   pl. رَوَابِط (root ر ب ط).

وَسیله   method   pl. وَسایِل (root و س ل).

Five-letter singulars use the plural form فَعَالیل.

These forms are as above, with the addition of a 'long' vowel, usually in the last syllable.

قانون   law   pl. قَوانین (root ق ن ن).

مَکتوب   letter   pl. مَکاتیب (root کـ ت ب).

أَحداث   news   pl. آحادیث[1] (root ح د ث).

(pl. of حَدَث novelty)

تَصویر   illustration   pl. تَصاویر (root ص و ر).

دُکّان   shop   pl. دَکاکین (root دکـ ن).

The Arabic Broken Plural is to some extent to be regarded as a collective noun rather than as a simple plural. For this reason it is quite common to find the regular Persian plural side by side with it, e.g. کُتُب and کِتابها.

---

[1] Generally used as plural of حَدیث, religious tradition.

Many of these plurals are more common in Persian than the corresponding singular. In certain cases they are used with a singular meaning.

أَرْباب master (sing. رَبّ—Lord (God)).

In such cases the broken plural 'collective' may itself take a Persian plural ending, e.g.

أَرْبابها masters.

(b) Nouns of Place and Time

These normally have the prefix ma-.

مَنزِل house (root ن ز ل alight).

مَدرَسه school (root د ر س study).

مَوقِع occasion (root وق ع fall).

(c) Nouns of Instrument

These often have the prefix me-.

مِفتاح key (root ف ت ح open).

مِسواكْ toothbrush (root س و كْ rub).

(d) Trades and occupations have the form فَعّال.

نَقّاش painter (root ن ق ش draw, engrave).

بَقّال grocer (root ب ق ل grow (of plants)).

فَرّاش messenger (root ف ر ش spread (carpet)).

نَجّار carpenter (root ن ج ر hew (wood)).

106. Verb Formulae

The only parts of the Arabic verbal conjugation that affect Persian are the two Participles (Active and Passive) and the Verbal Noun. The situation is however complicated by the fact that from any given root up to sixteen different verbs may be formed according to set formulae, each giving a different shade of meaning. In practice only nine of these forms are common, and few if any roots are known to have all of them.

Before giving the distinctive forms of the participles and verbal nouns of each of these 'derived' verbs, a note is necessary on the general significance of each.

I. The simple form of the verb.

II. Intensive, sometimes causative.

III. Attempt; reciprocity.

IV. Causative.

V. Reflexive of II; often passive in sense.

VI. Reflexive of III.

VII. Passive.

VIII. Reflexive of I.

X.[1] Reflexive of IV; asking, desiring, claiming.

It should be understood that these modifications of meaning cannot be taken to operate automatically. The above notes are intended only as a guide.

(a) Participles (A. = active; P. = passive.)

		Form	Example	Meaning	Root	Root meaning
I	A.	فاعـل	شاعـر	poet	ش ع ر	versify
	P.	مَفعول	مَكتوب	letter	كت ت ب	write
II	A.	مُفَعِّل	مُفَتِّش	inspector	ف ت ش	inspect
	P.	مُفَعَّل	مُثَلَّث	triangular	ث ل ث	three
III	A.	مُفاعِل	مُعاوِن	assistant	ع و ن	help
	P.	مُفاعَل	مُبارَك	blessed	ب ر ك	lie down
IV	A.	مُفعِل	مُخبِر	correspondent	خ ب ر	inform
	P.	مُفعَل	مُحكَم	strong	ح كت م	be wise, firm
V	A.	مُتَفَعِّل	مُتَخَصِّص	expert	خ ص ص	be special
	P.	مُتَفَعَّل	مُتَرَقَّب	expected	ر ق ب	watch
VI	A.	مُتَفاعِل	مُتَحارِب	belligerent	ح ر ب	fight
	P.	مُتَفاعَل	—	—	—	—[2]
VII	A.	مُنفَعِل	مُنعَكِس	reflected	ع كت س	reverse
	P.	مُنفَعَل	—	—	—	—[2]
VIII	A.	مُفتَعِل	مُنتَظِر	awaiting	ن ظ ر	look

[1] Form IX is rare in Persian.
[2] The passive form is rare in these cases.

P.	مُفْتَعَل	مُنْتَظَر	awaited	ن ظ ر	look
X A.	مُسْتَفْعِل	مُسْتَخْدِم	employee	خ د م	serve
P.	مُسْتَفْعَل	مُسْتَحْكَم	solid	ح كۡ م	be wise, firm

It will be seen that in all but Form I, the only difference between the two Participles is the vowel-change in the last syllable.

(b) Verbal Noun

Form		Example	Meaning	Root	Root meaning
I	Irregular	قَتْل	murder	ق ت ل	kill
		شكَايَت	complaint	ش كۡ و	complain
		قَبُول	acceptance	ق ب ل	accept
II		تَفْعيل تَعْطيل	holiday	ع ط ل	be idle
III	(a)	مُفَاعَله مُلاحَظه	consideration	ل ح ظ	look at
	(b)	فِعال وِصال	union, connection	و ص ل	join
IV		إفْعال إخْراج	expulsion	خ ر ج	go out
V		تَفَعُّل تَصَوُّر	imagination	ص و ر	shape
VI		تَفاعُل تَصادُف	collision	ص د ف	meet
VII		إنْفِعال إنْحِصار	monopoly	ح ص ر	surround
VIII		إفْتِعال إشْتِباه	mistake	ش ب ه	resemble
X		إسْتِفْعال إسْتِعْمال	use	ع م ل	work

107. Irregular Forms

When one or more of the root letters is *hamze*, و or ی, contractions and changes may take place in these forms. A few examples will serve to illustrate the general effect of these.

Para. 105:

(a) أَيّام days, from یوم day (root ی و م), for [أَیْوام].

آبْنا sons, from اِبْن son (root ب ن ی), for [أَبْنای].

مَبانی principles, from مَبْنی basis (root ب ن ی), for [مَبانِیْ].

(b)   مَقام   position, from root م و ق stand, for [مَقَوَم].

(c)   مِرآت   mirror, from root أ ى ر see, for [مِرأَيَة].

(d)   بَنّا   mason, from root ب ن ى build, for [بَنّاى].

Para. 106:

(a)   قاضى   judge, for [قاضِو] (root ق ض و decide).

مَبنى   based, for [مَبنوى] (root ب ن ى build).

مَخوف   frightened, for [مَخووف] (root خ و ف fear).

مُدير   director, for [مُدور] (root د و ر turn).

مُنشى   clerk, for [مُنشِىُ] (root ن ش ء grow, happen).

مُجاز   allowed, for [مُجوَز] (root ج و ز cross).

مُتَمَنّى[1]   requested, for [مُتَمَنّىْ] (root م ن ى determine).

مُتَلاشى   decomposing, for [مُتَلاشِو] (root ل ش و become corrupt).

مُبتَدى   beginner, for [مُبتَدِئ] (root ب د ء begin).

مُبتَلا   afflicted, for [مُبتَلَو] (root ب ل و afflict).

مُحتاج   needed, for [مُحتَوَج] (root ح و ج need).

مُستَقيم   direct, for [مُستَقوِم] (root ق و م stand).

مُستَشار   counsellor, for [مُستَشوَر] (root ش و ر test).

(b)   تَربِيَت   education, for [تَربِيو(تَ)] (root ربو grow up).

مُجازات   punishment, for [مُجازَيَت] (root ج ز ى requite).

اطاعَت   obedience, for [اطواع(تَ)] (root ط و ع obey).

تَرَقّى   progress, for [تَرَقُّى] (root ر ق ى ascend).

تَساوى   equality, for [تَساوُى] (root س و ى be equivalent).

اِنقِضا   end, for [اِنقِضاو] (root ق ض و decide, determine).

اِبتِدا   beginning, for [اِبتِداء] (root ب د ء begin).

اِحتِياج   desire, for [اِحتِواج] (root ح و ج need).

---

[1] ى is sometimes used to represent a final a sound (see para. 57, note).

اِسْتِعْفا resignation, for [اِسْتِعْفاو] (root ع ف و pardon).

اِسْتِيلا conquest, for [اِسْتِولاى] (root و ل ى rule).

اِسْتِقامَت resistance, for [اِسْتِقوام(-َت)] (root ق و م stand).

Other changes take place when the second and third letters of the root are the same.

دالّ pointing to, for [دالِل] (root د ل ل indicate) I.

مُنْحَلّ dissolved, for [مُنْحَلِل] (root ح ل ل loosen) VII.

مُسْتَقِلّ independent, for [مُسْتَقلِل] (root ق ل ل few) X.

The ت inserted into the VIIIth form assimilates to a greater or less degree to other dental consonants, and to the Arabic 'emphatic' consonants ص, ض, ط, ظ, and also absorbs و.

مُتَّهَم suspected, for [مُوْتَهَم] (root و ه م fancy).

مُدَّعى claimant, for [مُدْتَعو] (root د ع و call).

مُزْدَحَم crowded, for [مُزْتَحَم] (root ز ح م crowd).

مُضْطَرَب disturbed, for [مُضْتَرَب] (root ض ر ب strike).

مُطَّلِع informed, for [مُطْتَلِع] (root ط ل ع rise).

اِصطِلاح idiom, for [اِصْتِلاح] (root ص ل ح correct).

108. Other Arabic Usages

Certain other Arabic usages are found from time to time in Persian.

(a) The Definite Article

The word for 'the' in Arabic is اَل. It appears in Persian only in a considerable number of names, and in certain expressions borrowed complete. It also forms the first half of the word اَللّٰه God (pronounced *allah*, the short stroke above the *tašdid* standing for *alef*). The chief points to be noted are:

(i) The *fathe* is absorbed by any preceding vowel.

(ii) The *lam* is assimilated to a following ت ,ث ,د ,ذ ,ر ,ز ,س ,ش ,ص ,ض ,ط ,ظ ,ل, and ن, i.e. the following letter receives a *tašdid*. However, the redundant *alef* and *lam* are preserved in the writing.

عَبدُ النَّبِى   Abdo-n-Nabi.

عَبَدُ الرَّحِيم   Abdo-r-Rahim.

نَصرُ الدِّين   Nasro-d-Din.

ماوَرایَ النَّهر   (*ma-varaya-n-nahr*) Transoxania
                        (lit. 'what [is] beyond the river').

but   عَبَدُ المَجَید   Abdo-l-Majid.

The *alef* of the article is always written, even when the sound is absorbed by a preceding vowel, except after the Arabic preposition ل to.

بِالحَقیقه in truth (*belhaqiqe*);   بِالآخِره in the end (*belaxere*);

but آلحَمدُ لِلّٰه (the) praise [be] to God! (*al-hamdo lellah*).

(b) The Feminine Ending

The Arabic Feminine ending, occurring as a basic part of some words, and also used in the inflection of adjectives and nouns, is ة... (*-atun*). In Persian this may be modified either to ه... or to ـَت... ; sometimes the same word may occur with both forms, with or without modification of meaning.

اِداره office   (Ar. اِدارَة).

فُرصَت opportunity (Ar. فُرصَة).

Plural words in Arabic, whether of the 'Broken' (see para. 105 above) or 'Sound' (see para. 108 (*c*) below) type, are regarded in Arabic as feminine singular (except when they refer to persons). So in Persian too an Arabic adjective qualifying an Arabic plural may often take the Arabic feminine ending:

دُوَل مُتَّحِده The United Nations.

تَرتیبات لازِمه the necessary arrangements.

(c) Arabic case-endings

These are confined to (i) the Dual ...ـَين, used in certain expressions such as والِدَين (two) parents; طَرَفَين the two parties.

(ii) the Sound Plural endings ...ین (masc.) and ...ات (fem.) (see para. 28(b)):

مَأمورین   officials.

سُؤالات   questions.

(iii) The Accusative ending ...اً or ً (... an), used adverbially (see para. 57):

تَقریباً   nearly.

حَقیقةً   truly.

EXERCISES

A. Translate into English:

تا این آواخرِ در ایران تماشاخانه وجود نَداشت و نمایش بمعنی امروزیِ این کلمه بر ایرانیان مجهـول بود. از اوایلِ قرن بیستم ایرانیـان کمَ کَم شروع بترجمهٔ نمایشنامه‌های نَویسندگان غرب نمودنـد، ولی این آثار بیشتر برای مطالعه بدرد میخورد وراجع بآنها نمایشی بترتیب داده نمیشد. کَم کَم دسته‌هایِ کوچکِ بـازیگران تشکیل شده پاره ای از هین نمایشنامه‌ها بازی کردند و رفته رفته ذَوقی در مردم برای تماشای نمایش ایجاد شد. امروز گَذشته از عدهٔ زیادی سینماهای بزرگِ که در تهران و دیگر شهرها با وسایل جدید دایر است دسته‌های بازیگر در تهران و سایر جاها تشکیل شده و در پایتخت هنرستان مخصوصی برای تهیهٔ بازیگران تأسیس شده است. از طرف دیگر چند سال است که هنرستان عالی موسیقی تأسیس شده وتحت نظر استادان اروپائی یا ایرانی نوازندگان و خوانندگان و موسیقی دانهای لازم را تهیه میکند.

B. Translate into Persian:

Though during the nineteenth century A.D. Persia lost a large part of her land to Russia, Afghanistan and the Ottoman Empire, from another point of view it was a period of stability and consolidation. Above all it witnessed the influence of western ideas and industrial techniques. Many students began to travel in Europe for education, and at the same time numerous concessions were granted to European companies for the discovery and exploitation of Persia's natural resources. The impact of these events on Persian society led to a demand on the part of the people for a greater share in the government of the country, which demand culminated in the granting of a constitution in 1324 A.H. (lunar). In the years after the First World War the Qajar dynasty was deposed by Reza Khan, who crowned himself (placed the crown on his own head) as the first Shah of the Pahlavi dynasty, and inaugurated a vigorous programme of reform and modernization. The Anglo-Russian invasion of 1320 A.H. (solar) during the Second World War forced his abdication, but, on the foundation he had laid, the peaceful establishment of a constitutional democracy under the guidance of his son Mohammad Reza Shah became possible.

VOCABULARY

theatre	تَماشاخانه	be suitable	بِدَرد خُوردَن
play (n.)	نَمایِش، نَمایِشنامه	in connection with	راجِع به
meaning	مَعنی	arrange	تَرتیب دادَن
word	کَلِمه	group	دَسته
unknown	مَجهول	player	بازیگَر
first parts	آوایِل	be formed	تَشکیل شُدَن
translation	تَرجَمه	portion	پاره
write	نَوِشتَن (نَویس)	play, act (v.)	بازی کَردَن
west	غَرب	gradually	رَفته رَفته
effect (pl. آثار works)	اَثَر	taste	ذَوق
reading	مُطالَعه	watching	تَماشا
more	بیشتَر	apart from	گُذَشته اَز

number	عِدّه	numerous	مُتَعَدّد
cinema	سینِما	grant	واگُذار کَردَن
in operation, running	دایِر	discovery	اِکتِشاف
rest, remainder	سایِر	exploitation	اِستِثمار
academy	هُنَرِستان	resource (pl مَنابِع)	مَنبَع
training	تَهیِه	impact	بَرخُورد
music	موسیقی	society	اِجتِماع
under	تَحت	lead to	مُنجَرّ شُدَن به
supervision	نَظَر	demand	تَقاضا
play (instrument)	نَواختَن (نَواز)	on the part of	از طَرَف
sing	خواندَن	share	سَهم
although	آگَرچه	government	حُکومَت
lose	از دَست دادَن	culminate	خاتِمه یافتَن
Russia	روسیه	granting	اِعطا
Afghanistan	آفغانِستان	constitution(al)	مَشروطه
point of view	نُقطهٔ نَظَر	lunar	قَمَری
stability	ثَبات	war	جَنگ
consolidation	اِستِحکام	depose	مَعزول کَردَن
above all	از هَمه بالاتَر	Pahlavi	پَهلَوی
witness (v.)	مُشاهَده کَردَن	crown	تاج
influence	نُفوذ	place, lay	گُذاردَن
technique (pl. آسالیب)	أُسلوب	head	سَر
industrial	صَنعَتی	vigorous	شَدید
student (pl. ...ین)	مُحَصِّل	reform	اِصلاح
education	تَعلیم و تَربیَت	programme	بَرنامه
at the same time	دَر عَینِ حال	modernization	تَجَدُّد
concession (pl. اِمتیازات)	اِمتیاز	inaugurate	اِفتِتاح نَمودَن

solar	شَمسی	establishment	تَشکیل
abdication	اِستِعفا	peaceful	صُلح آمیز
force (v.)	تَحمیل نَمودَن	democracy	دِموکراسی
foundation	آساس	guidance	هِدایَت

APPENDIX A

The Nastaʔliq Script

1. The *nastaʔliq* variant of the Arabo-Persian script came into use in Persia during the fifteenth century, and since that time has been used almost exclusively for the writing of manuscripts in the Persian language. It continued to be used for the production of books by the lithographic process when this was introduced into Persia in the middle of the nineteenth century. Towards the end of the century letterpress printing began to gain ground; owing to the different levels at which *nastaʔliq* letters have to be joined, it was found impracticable to devise a satisfactory *nastaʔliq* typeface, and consequently the *nasx* type has been used almost entirely since that date for the printing of books and newspapers.

The *nastaʔliq* script, however, is still used (by photographic reproduction) for artistically printed books, as well as for book titles, display advertisements, shop signs, street names, posters, etc., so that a knowledge of it is essential. Moreover, it forms the basis of the *šekaste* script (Appendix B), which is the universal handwriting form now used for letters and so on.

2. The main characteristic of the *nastaʔliq* script that distinguishes it from the *nasx* is the fact that the letters slope backwards instead of forwards—that is, in a downward direction from right to left. Similarly combinations of letters tend to slope downwards in the same way (though to compensate for this, each successive combination tends to start *above* the preceding one). Coupled with this is a tendency to use a thicker pen in proportion to the size of letter, which has the further effect of exaggerating the broad strokes and elements in the letters, and minimizing the smaller details.

3. Table I gives the separate and joined forms of the letters in their *nasx* and *nastaʔliq* variants.

TABLE I

nastaʿliq	nasx
ا ا ا	ا ا
ب ب ب ب	ب ٮ ٮ ٮ
ح ح ح ح	ح ح ح ح
د ل	د د
ر ر	ر ر
س س ش س سس سس	س س س س س س
ص ص ص ص	ص ص ص ص
ط ط ط ط	ط ط ط ط
ع ع ع ع	ع ء ء ء
ف ف ف ق	ف ٯ ڡ ق ق
ک ک ک ک	ک ک ک ک
ل ل ل ل	ل ل ل ل
م م م م	م م م م
ه ه ه ه	ه ه ه ه
	ق و
	ن ن
	ى ى

Points to be especially noted are:

(i) the forms assumed by د, لـ . . . . ر, ر . . . . ر, رو, و . . . . ر,
all of which are easily confused.

(ii) the two forms of س (in both separate and joined forms). In
general the long stroke is used when there are no other long strokes
(e.g. letters of the ب form) in the particular combination.

(iii) the various forms of ه, and especially the initial form.

4. Letters in combination undergo similar modifications to those
observed in the *nasx* script, with a tendency still further to smooth away
sharp angles. The more significant combinations are illustrated in
Table II.

TABLE II

Combined forms in *nasx* and *nastaʔliq* compared

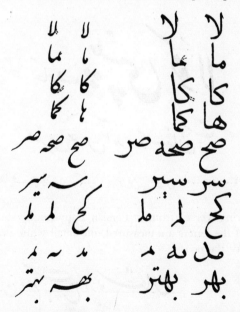

5. The only writing signs that differ at all in appearance are *hamze* and
madde.

6. The following short examples serve to illustrate some of the points mentioned. It will be seen that the dots, being written with the full thickness of the pen, are larger in proportion to the letters than in *nasx*, as well as being placed further away and less exactly in relation to the letter to which they belong.

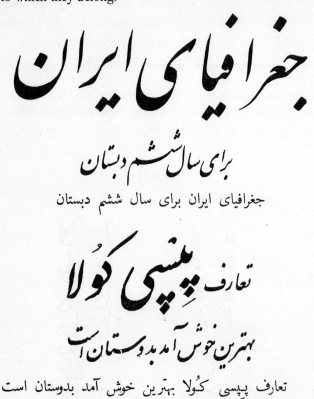

جغرافیای ایران

جغرافیای ایران برای سال ششم دبستان

تعارف پپسی کولا

تعارف پپسی کولا بهترین خوش آمد بدوستان است

The following verse, from a Persian copy-book, shows how the proportions of the letters are measured, the small white dots being each the thickness of the pen.

بود چون دم صبح در بوستان

نصیحتگری بر دل دوستان

Notes: بُوَد is an archaic form of the Subjunctive of بودن, here used with a general or timeless sense.

In verse the order of words frequently differs from the natural prose order.

VERBATIM TRANSLATION

> 'Is like the breath of morning in the garden
> Wise-counsel upon the heart of friends.'

The two passages that follow are the Persian exercises from Lessons x and xi (with one or two minor modifications). No transcription is therefore given here.

LESSON X

آب و هوای ایران

ایران ما در منطقهٔ معتدل شمالی قرار دارد و بدین سبب آب و هوای آن بطور کلی

معتدل است، اما به علت کوههای بلند و گسترده و صحراهای پهنا ور و مجاورت

دریاها انواع گوناگون آب و هوای معتدل در آن می بینیم چنانکه در کناره های

دریای مازندران آب و هوا معتدل و بارانی ، در صحراهای داخلی گرم و خشک

در کوهستانها سرد و در کناره های جنوب بسیار گرم است . پرباران ترین

جای ایران کناره های دریای مازندران و خشک ترین ناحیهٔ آن کویر لوت

است .

LESSON XI

نجات ماه

شب مهتابی در چاه نگاه میکرد عکس ماه را در چاه دید فکر کرد که ثواب دارد اگر ماه را از چاه

نجات دهد پس قلابی در چاه انداخته چند دور گردانید از قضا قلاب بسنگ بزرگی در ته چاه

گیر کرد ملا هر چه زور زد که آن را بالا بکشد از جای خود نکان نخورد آخر الامر از نفس قوّت کرد

ریسمان پاره شد ملا به پشت افتاد و چون نگاه کرد ماه را در آسمان دید گفت : عیب ندارد

اگر چه خیلی رنج کشیدم ولی بمقصد رسیده ماه را نجات دادم .

APPENDIX B

The Šekaste Script

1. The *šekaste* or 'broken' script is a derived form of the *nastaʔliq*, its main characteristic, apart from those shared with its parent script, being the linking up of letters that are not normally joined. The tendency towards minimization and exaggeration already noted in the *nastaʔliq* script is carried still further, as is the smoothing out of sharp curves and angles.

Since nowadays it is normally written with a steel or fountain pen, instead of the traditional reed still used for the other two calligraphic scripts, it does not show the variations of thickness that are characteristic of *nasx* and *nastaʔliq*, and also of earlier *šekaste*. It must also be remembered that, unlike the other two scripts, it is an unstandardized handwriting, and therefore subject to the personal variations and idiosyncracies of individual writers. As will be seen even from the few examples given in this appendix, these variations can be very wide-ranging. No hard and fast rules can therefore be given, and the forms of the letters and combinations given below should be taken rather as a guide to the decipherment of hand-written letters. A further difficulty arises from the fact that many common terms and expressions used in correspondence are taken for granted, and so often scribbled without much attention to clarity. Fluency in recognizing these can only be acquired by constant practice.

2. In the first of the tables below the shapes of the individual letters are given in their joined and separate forms. Table II shows samples of letters in combination, while Table III shows combined groups of letters that are not joined in the standard scripts.

TABLE I

The *šekaste* alphabet

TABLE II

Some combined letters in *šekaste*

مد — سد — بین — یقین — یک — کمک — ملک — یگانه — لا — ملا — ح

بل — علل — سب — در — ظهر — ها — بهم — هم — کبه — یکی — اصلی

بک — عسر — سب — ظهر — بها — هم — فی — اصح

It should be noted that two dots are normally written as a short stroke, and three dots as a circle. Sometimes the final stroke of the letter or word is carried on so as to link the dot group to it.

شما: هم | است: است

Dots are correctly placed above or below the word, but rarely in closer relation to the letter itself; they are frequently omitted altogether. A group of three or more dots belonging to different neighbouring letters may often be combined in one circle.

انتظار: انتظار | مفتخراً: مفخوراً

TABLE III

'Separate' letters in combination

Alef joined to following letter.	*Re, Zein, Že* joined to following letter.

اند	اند	بقرا	فقرا
این	این	کرا	کرا
اده	اده	زاد	زاد
اده	اده	اراده	اراده
اد	اد	خواب	خواب
حاصل	حاصل	زیراکه زیراکه	زیراکه
آقای	آقای	زد	زد
مال	مال	دارد	دارد
اعلام	اعلام	کردن	کردن
		مردم	مردم
		پرده	پرده
		دک	دک
		فرموده	فرموده
		فرمان	فرمان
		سازمان	سازمان
		بالاخره	بالاخره
		ریا	ریا

See also *re, vav*.

Dal, Zal joined to following letter.

دم	دم
دق	دق
ده	ده
بده	بده
شده	شده
دیده	دیده

See also *alef, re, vav*.

Vav joined to following letter.

آورد آورلهه
آورده آورلهه
خورد خلهه
وَل وو
معلول معسب
تومان نمان
قانون قنّین
کوناکون لگا گن
جلوه جلوه

See also *re*.

وَا وَا
نَوا نَلا
خواهد خواهد
جوانان جوانان
انواع انواع
مطلوب مطلوب
وجهه وجه
وجوه وجوه
نبوده نبوده
نموده نموده

3. The three letters that follow are given primarily as samples of different styles of hand-writing. An exact transcription in *nasx* follows each, and careful note should be made of the modifications the letters have undergone. Apart from the script, the letters are also to be noted for their use of 'honorific' phraseology, which is characteristic even of comparatively informal letters.

آقای ساتن

متمنی است مقرر فرمائید در مقابل رسید آبونمان

جلد سوم مجلد آینده که به پیوست تقدیم میشود مبلغ

یکصد و پنجاه ریال به حامل لطف کنند .

TRANSCRIPTION

آقای ساتن

متمنی است مقرر فرمائید در مقابل رسید آبونمان جلد سوم مجله آینده
که به پیوست تقدیم میشود مبلغ یکصد وپنجاه ریال به حامل لطف کنند.

TRANSLATION

Mr Sutton

It is requested that you arrange (lit. 'order arranged') that, in exchange for the subscription receipt of the third volume of the magazine *ayande* (*The Future*) which is presented herewith, the bearer be given (lit. 'they do favour to the bearer') the sum of one hundred and fifty rials.

NOTES

فَرمودن, 'to order, command,' is commonly used in formal and semi-formal writing and conversation instead of the auxiliary verbs کردن, نمودن, etc., and also to replace گفتن. In all these cases it may only be used when the subject of the verb is the *person addressed*. The speaker or writer himself would either use the ordinary verbs or, as an alternative to گفتن, کردن, عَرض, 'to make a petition.'

لُطف کردن (passive تقدیم شدن) and تَقدیم داشتن both mean little more than 'to give', the first being used with the writer as subject, and the second for the addressee.

[handwritten Persian text]

TRANSCRIPTION

آقای ل.پ. الول ساتن عزیز

در جواب نامهٔ مورخ ۲۸ تیرماه ۱۳۲۶ جنابعالی بطوری که مرقوم
فرموده بودید با این نامه خلاصه‌ای از شرح حال و آثار خود را بضمیمهٔ
یک قطعه عکس تقدیم می‌دارم و ازینکه نام ارادتمند را هم در کتاب
خود راجع بترقی و پیشرفت مطبوعات ایران که قطعاً اثر بسیار نفیسی
خواهد بود ذکر خواهید کرد قبلاً صمیمانه تشکر می کنم.

ارادتمند

TRANSLATION

Dear Mr L. P. Elwell-Sutton

    In answer to your letter (lit. 'the letter of the lofty side') dated
28 Tirmah 1326, as you had written, with this letter I present a summary
of my biography and works, together with one (piece) photograph, and
I sincerely thank you in advance for the fact that you will mention my
name (lit. 'the name of the sincere [friend]') also in your book about the
progress and advancement of the press of Iran, which will certainly be
a very valuable work.

                                Sincerely,

NOTES

جَنابِعالی, lit. 'the lofty side', is the usual formal expression for
'you'. The corresponding phrases for 'I' are اینجانِب ('this side'), بَنده
('slave'), اِراد تَمَند ('sincere'), etc.

قِطعه is a numerator, see para. 88.

مرقوم فرموده بودید : see notes on preceding letter.

بمبئی ۲۲ دسامبر ۱۹۴۷

عزیز و محترم   امیدوارم و جوشرقه عکی

درحال صحت ا   خاصتم که درمند زلا مامدم

که شیر نفیض زمار سامان کرم

الغول حول عید یی نفذ نودک ا

ران نو شبکات حمد الفدیم داسه سلطت

الخ رامه ساکن و مسی و لعد ا را اکرا

الادلم محمد

TRANSCRIPTION

بمبئی ۲۲ دسامبر ۱۹٤۷

آقای عزیز ومحترم   امیدوارم وجــود شریف عالی در کمـــال
صحّت است   خیلی متاسفم که در لندن زیاد نماندم که بیشتر بفیض
زیارت شما نائل گردم.

اکنون چون عید سال نو نزدیک است تبریکات خود را تقدیم داشته
سلامت و سعادت شما را خواهانم.

یکماهی در بمبئی هستم وبعد بایران میروم.

فرمایشی باشد مرقوم فرمائید.

ارادتمند صمیمی

TRANSLATION

Bombay, 22 December 1947

Dear and respected Sir,

I hope (lit. 'am hopeful') you are (lit. 'the noble lofty existence is') in
good (lit. 'the perfection of') health. I am very sorry that I did not stay
long (lit. 'much') in London, so that I might more enjoy (lit. 'become
grasping at the bounty of') a visit to you.

Now, since the festival of the New Year is near, I present my greetings,
and wish (lit. 'am wishing') your well-being and happiness.

I am one month in Bombay, and after I go to Persia.

[If] there is a request (lit. 'command'), write [it].

Very sincerely,

NOTES

وُجــود شَریــف عالی: a rather elaborate honorific form, as also,
lower, بِفَیْضِ زِیارَتِ شُما نائل گَردم.

نائل, also فرمائید below: . ءَ . is used for . ءَ . . .

گردم : the extra stroke of the *gaf* is omitted.

خواهان: Present Participle of خواستن, 'to wish', see para. 99 *f.*

فرمائش: an alternative somewhat archaic spelling of فَرمایش, verbal noun from فَرمودن, 'to command', here—'to request' (see para. 99 *d*).

In the last two or three lines most of the dots are missing.

APPENDIX C

Books for Further Study and Reading

Language

G. Lazard: *Grammaire du Persan Contemporain* (Paris, 1957).

J. T. Platts and G. S. A. Ranking: *A Grammar of the Persian Language*, 2nd ed. (Oxford, 1911).

D. C. Phillpott: *Higher Persian Grammar* (Calcutta, 1919).

J. A. Boyle: *A Practical Dictionary of the Persian Language* (London, 1949).

S. Haim: *New Persian–English Dictionary*, 2 vols. (Tehran, 1934–36).

S. Haim: *Shorter Persian–English Dictionary* (Tehran, 1958).

S. Haim: *Larger English–Persian Dictionary*, 2 vols. (Tehran, 1941–3).

S. Haim: *One-volume English–Persian Dictionary* (Tehran, 1959).

S. Haim: *Shorter English–Persian Dictionary* (Tehran, 1959).

F. Steingass: *A Comprehensive Persian–English Dictionary* (London, 1892, repr. 1930).

H. D. Graves Law: *Persian Letters* (London, 1948).

Background

L. P. Elwell-Sutton: *Modern Iran* (London, 1941).

L. P. Elwell-Sutton: *Guide to Iranian Area Study* (Ann Arbor, 1952).

Donald Wilber: *Iran, Past and Present*, 4th ed. (Princeton, 1958).

Olive Suratgar: *I Sing in the Wilderness* (London, 1951).

Sir Percy Sykes: *History of Persia*, 2 vols., 3rd ed. (London, 1930).

R. Ghirshman: *Iran* (Harmondsworth, 1954).

R. Roolvink: *Historical Atlas of the Muslim Peoples* (Amsterdam, 1957).

R. Levy: *The Social Structure of Islam*, 2nd ed. (Cambridge, 1957).

D. M. Donaldson: *The Shi'ite Religion* (London, 1933).

A. J. Arberry (ed.): *The Legacy of Persia* (Oxford, 1953).

A. A. Hekmat: *Glimpses of Persian Literature* (Calcutta, 1956).

R. Levy: *Persian Literature* (London, 1923).

A. J. Arberry: *Classical Persian Literature* (London, 1958).

E. G. Browne: *Literary History of Persia*, 4 vols., 2nd ed. (Cambridge, 1928).

M. Ishaque: *Modern Persian Poetry* (Calcutta, 1943).

M. Rahman: *Post-Revolution Persian Verse* (Aligarh, 1955).

M. S. Dimand: *Handbook of Muhammadan Art*, 2nd ed. (New York, 1937).

Arthur Upham Pope: *Masterpieces of Persian Art* (New York, 1945).

A. T. Wilson: *Bibliography of Persia* (Oxford, 1930).

Suggested Reading in Persian

Kuhi Kermani: *Panzdah Afsaneye Rusta?i*. Folk Tales. (Tehran, 1954).

Iranian Ministry of Education: *Joqrafyaye Iran baraye Sale Šešome Dabestan*. School geography. (Tehran, 1958).

Mahdi Hamidi (ed.): *Daryaye Gouhar*, Vol. I. Modern short stories. (Tehran, 1950).

PERSIAN–ENGLISH VOCABULARY

N.B.—The following list contains all the words used in the Grammar, but in general the meanings given are only those appropriate to the particular usages in the examples and exercises.

ا

(see آمدن)	آ–	last	آخِرین
water	آب	lately	آخِراً
climate	آب و هَوا	literature	أدَبیّات
cultivated	آباد	office, department	إداره
Aban (8th month)	آبان	Âzar (9th month)	آذَر
beginning	إبتِدا	sincere	إراد تَمَند
alphabet	أبجَد	adornment	آرایش
cloud	أبر	adorn	آرایش دادن
son	إبن (pl. بَنی)	master	آرباب
subscription	آبونمان	(see رَبّ)	
blue	آبی	Ardashir (founder of Sasanid dynasty)	آردَشیر
irrigation	آبیاری	Ordibehesht (2nd month)	أردیبِهِشت
union, unity	إتّحاد	cheap	آرزان
bus	أتوبوس	Europe	أروپا
motor-car	أتومُبیل	European	أروپائی
effect, trace	أثَر (pl. آثار = works)	yes	آری
permission	إجازه	Aryan	آریائی
allow	إجازه دادن	from; than	آز
society	إجتِماع	foundation	آساس
(see جَدّ)	أجداد	easy	آسان
carry out	إجرا کَردَن	horse	آسب
need	إحتیاج (pl. إحتیاجات)	article(s)	أسباب
Ahmad (male name)	أحمَد	(see سَبَب)	
(see حال)	أحوال	toy	أسباب بازی
final(ly)	آخِر	Spain	إسپانیا
in the end	آخِرُ الأمر	master	أستاد
expulsion	إخراج	exploitation	إستِثمار
expel	إخراج کَردن	consolidation	إستِحکام
		abdication	إستِعفا

use	استعمال	most(ly)	اَغلَب
resistance	استقامَت	sun	آفتاب
reception	استقبال	fall	اُفتادَن (اُفت—)
receive (guests, etc.)	استقبال کردن	opening, inauguration	افتِتاح
studio	استودیو	inaugurate	افتِتاح نَمودن
conquest	استیلا	creation	آفَرینِش
(see سرّ)	اسرار	tale	اَفسانه
Alexander	اِسکَندَر	Afghan	اَفغان
Esfand (12th month)	اسفَند	Afghanistan	اَفغانِستان
Islam	اسلام	sir, Mr	آقا
Islamic	اسلامی	step, advance	اِقدام
technique	اُسلوب (pl. آسالیب)	at least	اَقَلّاً
name	اِسم	آکبَر (pl. آکابِر = adults)	
name (v.)	اِسم گُذاشتِن	elder; Akbar (Mogul emperor)	
Esma'il	اسماعیل	discovery	اِکتِشاف
sky	آسمان	majority	اَکثَریَت
Asia	آسیا	now	اَکنون
mistake	اِشتِباه	already	هَم اَکنون
make a mistake	اِشتِباه کردن	if	اَگَر
(see شَخص)	آشخاص	although	اَگَرچه
occupation	اِشغال	family	آل
occupy	اِشغال کردن	Buyids	آلِ بویه
Ashkanian, Parthian	آشکانی	Samanids	آلِ سامان
acquainted, acquaintance	آشنا	آلا— (see آلودَن)	
(see صاحِب)	آصحاب	now, directly	آلآن
insistence	اِصرار	certainly	اَلبَتّه
insist	اِصرار کردن	thanks be to God	اَلحَمدُ لِلّه
idiom	اِصطِلاح	God (Ar.)	اَللّه
Isfahan	اِصفَهان	stain	آلودَن (آلا—)
originally	اَصلاً	Elizabeth	اِلیزابِت
reform	اِصلاح	but	اَمّا
obedience	اِطاعَت	statistics, calculation	آمار
room	اُطاق	emperor	اِمپِراتور
strike (n.)	اِعتِصاب	empire	اِمپِراتوری
granting	اِعطا	examination	اِمتِحان
majesty	آعلَیحَضرَت	concession	اِمتِیاز (pl. اِمتِیازات)
anarchy, disorder	اِغتِشاش		

come	آمَدَن (آ—)	first	اوَّل
come out	بیرون آمدن	firstly	اوَّلاً
affair; order	آمر (اُمور .pl)	first	اوَّلین
order (v.)	امر دادن	Ahriman (Zoroastrian spirit of evil)	اهرِمَن
today	اِمروز	importance	اهَمِّیت
tonight	اِمشَب	iron	آهَن
possibility	اِمکان	*interrogative particle*	آیا
teach	آموختَن (آموز—)	(see یَوم)	اَیّام
teacher	آموزگار	creation	ایجاد
mix	آمیختَن (آمیز—)	create	ایجاد نَمودن
associate	دَر آمیختن	Iran, Persia	ایران
hope	امید	Iranian, Persian	ایرانی
hope (v.)	امید داشتن	stand	ایستادَن (ایست—)
hopeful	امیدوار	station	ایستگاه
(see آمیختَن)	آمیز—	they	ایشان
that	آن	tribe	ایل (ایلات .pl)
store	اَنبار	this	این
there	آنجا	here	اینجا
monopoly	اِنحصار	coming, future	آیَنده
throw	اَنداختَن (اَنداز—)		
little	اَندَک		
justice	اِنصاف		
unjust	بی اِنصاف		**ب**
(see نَظَر)	اَنظار	with, by	با
end	اِنقضا	(see بایستَن)	با—
then	آنگاه	gate	باب
England, Britain	اِنگلیستان	papa	بابا
English, British	اِنگلیسی	wind	باد
stir up	اَنگیختَن (اَنگیز—)	time ('fois'); load	بار
he, she, it	او	once again	بار دیگَر
last parts	اَواخِر	rain (n.)	باران
middle parts	اَواسِط	rainy	پُرباران
first parts	اَوایِل	rainy	بارانی
zenith	اَوج	rain (v.)	باریدن
bring	آوَردَن	open, again	باز
bring out, produce	دَر آوردن	open (v.)	باز کردن
(see وَقت)	اَوقات	return	باز گَشتَن
		bazaar	بازار

arm	بازو	be manifested	بـروز شُدَن
play	بازی	big, great	بُزُرگ
play, act	بازی کردن	enough	بَس
toy	اَسباب بازی	so much	اَزبَس
player, actor	بازیگَر	bind, close	بَستَن (بَنـد –)
(see بودن)	باش–	many, much, very	بِسیار
garden	باغ	after, next, later	بَعد
gardener	باغبان	some	بَعضی
weave	بافتَن	grocer	بَقّال
above; height, stature	بالا	but, perhaps, or rather	بَلکه
finally	بـالآخِره	long, tall	بُلَند
in truth	بـالحَقیقه	raise up	بُلَند کردن
bank	بانک	yes	بَلی
lady	بانو	Bombay	بَمبئَی
belief	باوَر	construction, basis	بَنا
believe	باوَر کردن	on the basis of	بَنابَر
together	باهَم	(see بَستَن)	بَند–
(see هوش)	باهوش	slave ; I	بَنده
be necessary	بایِستَن (با –)	smell	بو
child	بَچّه	be	بودَن (باش –)
bad	بَد	garden	بوستان
bad-natured	بَدنِهاد	Buyid (Persian dynasty)	بویه
on	بَر	to, with, in, by	به
on	بَرروی	Bahman (11th month)	بَهمَن
on	بَرسَر	without	بی
meet	بَرخوردَن	desert	بیابان
pick up	بَرداشتَن	explanation	بَیان
return	بَرگَشتَن	verse	بَیت (pl. آبیات)
brother	بَرادَر	awake	بیدار
nephew	بَرادَر زاده	waken	بیدار کردن
for	بَرای	out, outside	بیرون
impact	بَرخورد	expel	بیرون کردن
carry, take away	بُردَن (بَر –)	twenty	بیست
snow	بَرف	more	بیش، بیشتَر
lightning, electricity	بَرق	ill	بیمار
flash (v.)	بَرق زدن	hospital	بیمار ستان
programme	بَرنامه	(see دیدن)	بین –

between	بَین	day after tomorrow	پسفَردا
among	مابَین	back (n.); behind (prep.)	پُشت
nose	بینی	five	پَنج
		fifty	پَنجاه
	پ	window	پَنجَره
		Thursday	پَنجشَنبه
foot	پا	hand	پَنجه
Papakan (family name of	پاپِکان	wear (clothes)	پوشیدَن
Ardashir, founder of Sasanid dynasty)		money	پول
king	پادشاه	Pahlavi (surname of reigning	پَهلَوی
Parthian	پارت (پارتها .pl)	dynasty in Persia)	
cloth	پارچه	wide	پَهن
portion	پاره	extensive	پَهناوَر
break, tear (v. intrans.)	پاره شدن	track; in pursuit of	پی
policeman	پاسبان	cup	پیاله
clean	پاک	twist, corner, screw	پیچ
fifteen	پانزدَه	evident	پیدا
five hundred	پانصَد	find	پیدا کردن
capital	پایتَخت	old (person)	پیر
down, below	پائین	shirt, blouse	پیراهَن
lower (v.)	پائین آوَردن	follower	پیرو
father	پدَر	victory	پیروزی
receive, accept	پَذیرُفتَن (پَذیر–)	near, in the presence of, 'chez'; ago	پیش
full	پُر	before	پیش از
rainy	پُرباران	go forward	پیش رَفتن
ask	پُرسیدَن	advancement	پیشرَفت
flight	پَرواز	prophet	پیغمبَر
fly	پَرواز کردن	union	پیوست
flying (adj.)	پَروازی	herewith, enclosed	به پیوست
Parviz (male name)	پَرویز		
Parvin (female name)	پَروین		ت
day before yesterday	پَریروز	until, as far as; as long as, so that	تا
night before last	پَریشَب	fold, unit	تا
after, behind; then	پَس	theatre	تیآتر
give back	پَس دادن	crown	تاج
post office	پُستخانه	history	تاریخ
son, boy	پیسَر	prehistoric	قَبل از تاریخ

H

fresh, new	تازه	imagination	تَصَوُّر
foundation	تَأسیس	imagine	تَصَوُّر کردن
found	تَأسیس کردن	picture, image (pl. تَصاویر)	تَصویر
fever	تَب	offering	تَعارُف
greeting	تَبریک (. . . ات .pl)	surprise	تَعَجُّب
commercial	تِجارَتی	be surprised	تَعَجُّب کردن
modernization	تَجَدُّد	holiday	تَعطیل
under	تَحت	teaching	تَعلیم
contempt	تَحقیر	education	تَعلیم وتَربیَت
humble (v.)	تَحقیر کردن	understanding	تَفاهُم
compulsion	تَحمیل	subtraction	تَفریق
force (v.)	تَحمیل نَمودن	demand	تَقاضا
throne, couch	تَخت	presentation	تَقدیم
Persepolis	تَختِ جَمشید	be presented	تَقدیم شدن
codification	تَدوین	present (v.)	تقدیم داشتن
codify	تَدوین کردن	nearly, about	تَقریباً
upbringing	تَربیَت	division	تَقسیم
arrangement	تَرتیب (تَرتیبات .pl)	fault	تَقصیر
arrange	تَرتیب دادن	moving	تَکان
translation	تَرجَمه	move (v. intrans.)	تَکان خُوردن
bitter, sour	تُرش	repetition	تِکرار
progress	تَرَقّی	be repeated	تِکرار شُدن
leaving	تَرک	alone	تَک وتَنها
leave (v. trans.)	تَرک کردن	bitter	تَلخ
Turkish	تُرکی	watching (n.)	تَماشا
equality	تَساوی	theatre	تَماشاخانه
ninth (fraction)	تُسع	all, whole	تَمام
Sirius	تیشتَر	civilization	تَمَدُّن
thanks	تَشَکُّر	body	تَن
thank (v.)	تشکر کردن	lazy	تَنبَل
establishment	تَشکیل	swift	تُند
be formed	تَشکیل شُدن	stenographer	تُندنِویس
encouragement	تَشویق	narrow, tight	تَنگ
encourage	تشویق کردن	tighten	تَنگ کردن
collision	تَصادُف	only, alone	تَنها
occupation	تَصَرُّف	loneliness	تَنهائی
occupy	تَصَرُّف کردن	thou, you (s.)	تُو

in (side)	تو	search (n.)	جُستُجو
powerful	تَوانا	geography	جُغرافیا
be able	تَوانِستَن (تَوان–)	pair	جُفت
by means of	تَوَسُّط	volume (book)	جِلد
expansion	تَوسِعه	meeting, session	جَلسه
expand (v. trans.)	تَوسِعه دادن	in front of	جِلَو
tuman (coin)	تومان	Jamshid (male name)	جَمشید
bottom	تَه	addition	جَمع
Tehran (capital of Persia)	تِهران	Friday	جُمعه
provision	تَهیه	side	جَناب
arrow; shaft, beam	تیر	your honour, you	جَنابِعالی
sharp	تیز	(lit. 'lofty side')	
Timur (male name)	تیمور	goods	جِنس (pl. آجناس)
Tamerlane	تیمورِ لَنگ	war	جَنگ
		fight	جَنگ کردن
ث		forest	جَنگَل
		south (n.)	جُنوب
secondly	ثانیاً	south (adj.)	جُنوبی
stability	ثَبات	barley	جو
wealth	ثَروَت	(see جُستَن)	جو–
rich	ثَروتمَند	answer	جَواب
third (fraction)	ثُلث	sack	جَوال
eighth (fraction)	ثُمن	young	جَوان
spiritual reward	ثَواب	sort, kind	جور
		jewel, essence, ink	جَوهَر (pl. جَواهِر)
ج		world	جَهان
		world (adj.)	جَهانی
place; instead of	جا	pocket	جیب
where	جائیکه		
because	از آنجائیکه	**چ**	
soul, life	جان		
side	جانِب	well	چاه
successor	جانِشین	tea	چای
animal	جانوَر	why?	چِرا
ancestor	جَدّ (pl. آجداد)	wheel	چَرخ
new	جَدید	eye	چَشم
except	جُز	wink	چَشمَک
seek	جُستَن (جو–)	spring	چَشمه

how?	چطَور	religious tradition (pl. آحادیث)	حَدیث
how much?	چقَدر	letter, word	حَرف
what sort of?	چگونه	speak	حَرف زَدن
such	چنان	movement	حَرَکَت
if	چنانچه	move, set out	حَرَکَت کردن
just as	چنانکه	feeling (pl. إحساسات)	حَسّ
some, how many?, how much?	چَند	Hasan (male name)	حَسَن
several, many	چَندان	Hosein (male name)	حُسَین
several	چَندین	preservation	حفظ
fork	چَنگال	truth, due	حَقّ
such	چُنین	grateful	حَقّ شِناس
wood, stick	چوب	really	حَقیقةً
how?, because, when, like	چون	story	حِکایَت
what?, because	چه	government, administration	حُکومَت
either . . . or	چه . . . چه	attack, invasion (pl. حَمَلات)	حَمله
four	چَهار	qualities	حَیثیات
fourteen	چَهارده		
Wednesday	چَهارشَنبه		
forty	چِهِلّ		
thing	چیز		

ح

خ

Haji, pilgrim	حاجی	end	خاتِمه
event, accident (pl. حَوادِث)	حادثه	culminate	خاتِمه یافتن
rich (fertile)	حاصلخیز	out (side)	خارِج
ready, present	حاضِر	go out	خارِج شُدن
condition (pl. آحوال)	حال	foreign(er)	خارِجی
whereas	دَر حالیکه	rise	خاستَن (خیز —)
until now	تابحال	rise up	بَرخاستن
biography	شَرح حال	earth	خاک
now	حالا	Khan	خان
bearer	حامِل	dynasty	خاندان
even	حَتّی	madam, Mrs, lady	خانُم
limit (pl. حُدود)	حَدّ	house	خانه
so far as . . ., to such an extent that	تاحَدّیکه	news (pl. آخبار)	خَبَر
		inform	خَبَر دادن
		bad (things)	خَراب
		Khorasan (province in N. E. Persia)	خُراسان
		Khordad (3rd month)	خُرداد

small quantity	خُرده	street	خیابان
purchaser	خَریدار	imagination	خیال
buy	خَریدَن	no	خیَر
tired	خَسته	(خاستن see)	خیز –
dry	خُشک	much, many, very	خیلی
blotting paper	خُشککُن		
angry	خَشمگین	**د**	
particularity	خُصوص		
especially	بخُصوص	in (side)	داخِل
line	خَطّ (pl. خُطوط)	internal	داخِلی
danger	خَطَر	give	دادَن (دِ ه –)
dangerous	خَطَرناک	(داشتن see)	دار –
summary	خُلاصه	Darius (Achaemenian king)	داریوش
Caliph	خَلیفه (pl. خُلَفا)	story	داستان
fifth (fraction)	خُمس	have	داشتَن (دار –)
sleep (n.)	خواب	pointing to	دالّ
bedroom	خوابگاه	skirt	دامَن
sleep (v.)	خوابیدَن	wise	دانا
wish, want, ask for	خواستَن (خواه –)	know	دانِستَن (دان –)
call, read, sing	خواندَن	grain, unit	دانه
(خواستن see)	خواه –	in operation, running	دایر
either … or	خواه … خواه	continually	دائماً
sister	خواهَر	primary school	دَبِستان
request (n.)	خواهِش	daughter, girl	دُختَر
request (v.)	خواهِش کردن	in	دَر
good	خوب	door	دَر
self	خُود	long	دَراز
eat, drink	خُوردَن	grade	دَرَجه
good	خُوش	tree	دَرَخت
welcome	خُوش آمَد	pain	دَرد
lucky	خُوشبَخت	be suitable	بِدَرد خُوردن
sweet-smelling	خُوشبو	lesson	دَرس
happiness	خُوشحالی	large, thick	دُرُشت
pretty	خُوشگِل	lie (n.)	دُروغ
happy	خُوشوَقت	sea	دَریا
blood	خون	thief	دُزد
self	خویش	steal	دُزدیدَن

hand; suit (of clothes)	دَست	late	دیر
lose	از دَست دادن	yesterday	دیروز
apparatus	دَستگاه	last night	دیشَب
instruction	دَستور (pl. دَستورات)	other	دیگَر
handle, group	دَسته	religion	دین
enemy	دُشمَن	dinar (small coin)	دینار
register, exercise book, office	دَفتَر	demon	دیو
time ('fois')	دَفعه	wall	دیوار
care, attention	دِقَّت		
minute	دَقیقه	**ذ**	
shop	دُکّان (pl. دَکاکین)		
doctor	دُکتُر	mention (n.)	ذِکر
heart	دِل	mention (v.)	ذِکر کردن
breath, mouth; at, near	دَم	taste	ذَوق
democracy	دِموکراسی		
two	دُو	**ر**	
twelve	دَوازدَه		
bicycle	دُو چَرخه	particle denoting direct object	را
sew	دوختَن (دوز—)	relation, connection	رابطه (pl. رَوابِط)
far	دور	in connection with	راجِع به
turn	دَور	comfortable	راحَت
telescope, camera	دوربین	true, right (hand)	راست
distant	دور دَست	pleased, content	راضی
period	دَوره	drive	راندَن
(see دوختَن)	دوز—	driver	رانَنده
friend	دوست	road	راه
love (v.)	دوست داشتَن	set out	راه اُفتادن
friendly	دوستانه	walk	راه رَفتَن
Monday	دُوشَنبه	railway	راه آهَن
government, state, nation	دَولَت (pl. دُوَل)	guidance	راهنَمائی
two hundred	دَویست	guide (v.)	راهنَمائی کردن
ten	دَه	Lord (رَبّ=master) (pl. آرباب)	رَبّ
village	دِه (pl. دِهات)	master	آرباب
villager	دِهاتی	quarter	رُبع
peasant	دِهقان	man	رَجُل
Dei (10th month)	دَی	rejection	رَدّ
see	دیدَن (بین—)	reject	رَدّ کردن

rule	رَسم
as, in the shape of	بَرسم
receipt	رَسِید
arrive	رَسِیدَن
sequence	رِشته
Reza (male name)	رِضا
conduct	رَفتار
behave	رَفتار کردن
go	رَفتَن (رَو—)
gradually	رَفته رَفته
removal	رَفع
companion	رَفیق
rival	رَقیب (رُقَبا .pl)
trouble	رَنج
take trouble	رَنج کردن
colour	رَنگ
coloured	رَنگین
face, on	رو
(رَفتن see)	رو—
(رابطه see)	رَوابط
circulation	رَواج
be current	رَواج داشتن
spread	رَواج یافتن
religious leader	(pl. ... ین) روحانی
river	رود(-خانه)
Rudaki (Persian poet)	رودَکی
day	روز
newspaper	روزنامه
(رئیس see)	رُؤَسا
rural	روستائی
Russian	روسی
Russia	روسیه
Roman, Greek	رومی
glory	رونَق
rial (coin)	رِیال
pour	ریختَن (ریز—)
pour out	بیرون ریختن

cord	ریسمان
manager	رئیس

ز

tongue, language	زَبان
knock, strike	زَدَن (زَن —)
gold	زَر
farming	زِراعَت
yellow	زَرد
Zoroaster	زَردُشت
Zoroastrian	زَردُشتی
clever	زَرَنگ
golden	زَرّین
reins	زِمام
time ('temps')	زَمان
winter	زِمِستان
ground, land, floor	زَمین
fall	زَمین خوردَن
(زَدن see)	زَن—
woman	زَن
Zand (18th century Persian dynasty)	زَند
life	زَندَگی
live	زَندَگی کردن
quick, soon	زود
strength	زور
exert oneself	زور زدَن
(زیستن see)	زی—
much, many, too much, too many, widely	زیاد
visit	زیارَت
harmful	زیانبَخش
beautiful	زیبا
under	زیر
because	زیرا
live	زیستَن (زی—)

س

past, former	سابِق
formerly	سابِقاً
make, build	ساختَن (ساز–)
simple	ساده
shore	ساحِل (سَواحِل .pl)
(ساختَن see)	ساز–
Sasanian (Persian dynasty)	ساسانی
hour, watch	ساعَت
year	سال
long years	سالیانِ دَراز
chieftain	سالار
Samanid (Persian dynasty)	سامان
rest	سایِر
cause	سَبَب (آسباب .pl)
article(s)	آسباب
because of	بِسَبَب
green	سَبز
seventh (fraction)	سُبع
entrust	سِپَردَن (سِپَر–)
then, next	سِپَس
star	سِتاره
magic	سِحر
difficult	سَخت
word	سُخَن
spokesman	سُخَنگو
poet	سُخَنوَر
sixth (fraction)	سُدس
head; on	سَر
end-to-end	سَرتاسَر (–ی)
secret	سِرّ (آسرار .pl)
soldier	سَرباز
red	سُرخ
cold (adj.)	سَرد
speed	سُرعَت

cold (n.)	سَرما
catch cold	سَرما خوردَن
upside down	سَرنِگون
overthrow	سَرنِگون کردن
surface	سَطح
happiness	سَعادَت
attempt (n.)	سَعی
try (v.)	سَعی کردن
white	سَفید
Safidrud (White River)	سَفیدرود
ceiling	سَقف
dog	سَگ
well-being	سَلامَت
Seljuq (Turkish dynasty)	سَلجوق
sultan, monarch	سُلطان
reign (n.)	سَلطَنَت
reign (v.)	سَلطَنَت کردن
Soleiman (male name)	سُلَیمان
Sindh	سِند
River Indus	رودِ سِند
stone	سَنگ
heavy	سَنگین
direction	سو
badness	سوء
misunderstanding	سوءِ تَفاهُم
suspicion, distrust	سوءِ ظَنّ
(ساحِل see)	سَواحِل
mounted	سَوار
mount (v. trans.)	سَوار کردن
mount (v. intrans.)	سَوار شُدن
question	سُؤال (سُؤالات .pl)
burn	سوختَن (سوز–)
hole	سوراخ
Syria	سوریه
(سوختَن see)	سوز–
three	سه

Tuesday	سه شَنبه
share	سَهم
thirty	سی
black	سیاه
apple	سیب
potato	سیب زَمینی
satisfied	سیر
soaked	سیراب
thirteen	سیزده
three hundred	سیصد
silver	سیم
cinema	سینما

ش

Shapur (male name)	شاپور
horn	شاخ
happiness	شادی
poet	شاعِر (pl. شُعَرا)
evening, supper	شام
sixteen	شانزده
Shah, king	شاه
prince	شاه زاده
achievement, masterpiece	شاهکار
royal	شاهَنشاهی
royal	شاهی
perhaps	شایَد
worthy	شایِسته
prevalent	شایِع
night	شَب
day and night	شَبان روز
camel	شُتُر
person	شَخص (pl. آشخاص)
personality	شَخصیَت (pl. ...ها)
become	شُدَن (شَو—)
vigorous	شَدید

explanation	شَرح
biography	شَرح حال
condition, term	شَرط (pl. شَرایِط)
east	شَرق
company	شِرکَت
participate	شِرکَت کردن
beginning	شُروع
begin	شُروع کردن
noble	شَریف
six	شِش
six hundred	شِشصَد
sixty	شَصت
(see شاعِر)	شُعَرا
penetrate	شِکافتَن
complaint	شِکایَت
complain	شِکایَت کردن
break, defeat	شِکَستَن (شِکَن—)
you	شُما
reckoning	شُمار
be reckoned	بِشُمار رفتن
number	شُماره
north	شِمال
northern	شِمالی
solar	شَمسی
recognize, know	شِناختَن (شِناس—)
acquainting (n.)	شِناسائی
identity card	شِناسنامه
Saturday	شَنبه
hear	شِنیدَن (شِنَو—)
(see شُدن)	شَو—
emotion	شور
highway	شوسه
Susa	شوش
driver	شوفِر
tragic	شوم
evidence	شِهادَت

town, city	شَهر
fame	شُهرَت
make one's name	شُهرَت یافتن
Shahrivar (6th month)	شَهریوَر
Shiraz	شیراز
Shirazi	شیرازی
sweet	شیرین
sweets	شیرینی
confectioner	شیرینی فُروش
Shi'a (sect of Islam)	شیعه

ص

owner, possessor (pl. آصحاب)	صاحِب
morning	صُبح
patience	صَبر
wait	صَبر کردن
health	صِحَّت
desert	صَحرا
hundred	صَد
shout, voice	صَدا
call	صَدا زَدن
Safavid (Persian dynasty)	صَفَوی
goodness	صَلاح
approve	صَلاح دانِستن
peace	صُلح
peaceful	صُلح آمیز
sincere	صَمیمانه
sincere	صَمیمی
(صَنعَت see)	صَنایع
fine arts	صَنایع ظَریفه
chair	صَندَلی
craft (pl. صَنایع)	صَنعَت
industrial	صَنعتی
form, face	صورَت
whereas; in case	دَر صورَتیکه
mask	صورَتَک

ض

blow; multiplication	ضَرب
contents	ضِمن
meanwhile	دَر ضِمن
annex (n.)	ضَمیمه
together with	بِضَمیمه

ط

naturally	طَبعاً
natural	طَبیعی
scheme	طَرح
side, direction	طَرَف
on the part of	اَز طَرَف
two sides	طَرَفَین
road (pl. طُرُق)	طَریق
demand (n.)	طَلَب
demand (v.)	طَلَب کردن
demand (v.)	طَلَبیدن
rising	طُلوع
rise	طُلوع کردن
rope	طَناب
manner	طَور
just as; so that	بِطوریکه، هَمانطوریکه
in general	بِطَور کُلّی
storm	طوفان
length	طول
last (v.)	طول کَشیدن
long	طولانی
aeroplane	طَیّاره

ظ

surface	ظاهِر
apparently	ظاهِراً
container	ظَرف
within, in the space of	دَر ظَرف

belief	ظَنّ
noon	ظُهر
appearance	ظُهور
appear	ظُهور یافتن

ع

just (adj.)	عادل
intelligent	عاقِل
lofty	عالی
generality	عامّه
accruing	عایِد
Abbas (male name)	عبّاس
Abdorrahim (male name)	عبدُ الرَّحیم
Abdolmajid (male name)	عبدُ المَجید
Abdonnabi (male name)	عبدُ النَّبی
Ottoman	عثمانی
for the time being	عِجالةً
haste	عَجَله
hurry	عَجَله داشتن
wonderful	عجیب
number	عَدَد
Iraq, Mesopotamia	عِراق
Arabs (coll.)	عَرَب
Arabia	عَرَبِستان
Arabic, Arabian	عَرَبی
petition	عَرض
say	عَرض کردن
dear	عَزیز
tenth (fraction)	عُشر
angry	عَصَبانی
evening; age	عَصر
behind	عَقَب
idea (pl. عَقایِد)	عَقیده
reflection	عَکس
cause	عِلَّت
Ali (male name)	عَلی

separately	عَلیَحِدّه
building	عِمارَت
uncle	عَمو
popular	عَوام پَسَند
fault	عَیب
it doesn't matter	عَیب نَدارَد
festival	عید
New Year gift	عیدی
eye; original	عَین
at the same time	در عَینِ حال

غ

cave	غار
careless	غافِل
west	غَرب
western	غَربی
submersion	غَرق
be submerged	غَرق شُدن
sunset	غُروب
strange(r)	غَریب
Ghazna (city in Afghanistan)	غَزنه
sorrow	غَمّ
sorrowful	غَمگین
other than	غَیر آز

ف

Persian (language)	فارسی
above	فَرا
envelop	فَراگِرفتن
messenger	فَرّاش
completion	فَراغَت
finish	فَراغَت یافتن
France	فَرانسه
tomorrow	فَردا
Ferdousi (Persian poet)	فِردَوسی

send	فرستادَن (فِرِست –)	height	قامَت
opportunity	فُرصَت	law	قانون (قَوانین .pl)
angel	فِرِشته	before; earlier	قَبل
order	فَرمودَن (فَرما–)	prehistoric	قَبل آز تاریخ
down	فُرو	in advance	قَبلاً
go down	فُرو رَفتَن	acceptance	قَبول
sell	فُروختَن (فُروش–)	accept	قَبول کردن
airport	فُرودگاه	murder	قَتل
Farvardin (1st month)	فَروَردین	stature	قَدّ
(فُروختَن see)	فُروش –	quantity	قَدر
culture	فَرهَنگ	power	قُدرَت
cultural	فَرهَنگی	old, ancient	قَدیم
shout (n.)	فَریاد	repose	قِرار
shout (v.)	فریاد زدن	establish	قِرار دادن
(فَریفتَن see)	فَریب –	be situated	قِرار داشتن
Faridun (male name)	فَریدون	restore	قِرار گُذاشتن
deceive	فَریفتَن (فَریب –)	be established	بَرقِرار شُدن
actually	فعلاً	century	قَرن (قُرون .pl)
only (adv.)	فَقَط	Middle Ages	قُرون وُسطیٰ
thought	فِکر	part	قِسمَت
think	فِکر کردن	chance	قَضا
plateau	فَلات	by chance	آز قَضا
technical	فَنّی	drop	قَطره (قَطَرات .pl)
immediately	فَوراً	cutting	قَطع
list	فَهرِست	be interrupted	قَطع شُدن
understanding	فَهم	certainly	قَطعاً
understand	فَهمیدَن	piece	قِطعه
bounty	فَیض	Caucasus	قَفقار
		lock (n.)	قُفل
	ق	lock (v.)	قُفل کردن
		hook	قِلاب
Qajar (Persian dynasty)	قاجار	fort	قَلعه
spoon	قاشُق	pen	قَلَم
magistrate, judge	قاضی	pencase	قَلَمدان
decisive	قاطِع	lunar	قَمَری
carpet	قالی	(قانون see)	قَوانین

strength	قُوَّت	general (adj.)	کُلّ
revive	قُوَّت دادن	hat	کُلاه
use force	قُوَّت کردن	word	کَلِمه
strong	قَوی	whole (adj.)	کُلّی
		in general	بِطَورِ کُلّی
	ک	little	کَم
		exceptional	کَم نَظیر
palace	کاخ	perfection	کَمال
(see کاشتن)	کار–	belt	کَمَربَند
work	کار	help	کُمَک
work (v.)	کار کردن	help (v.)	کُمَک کردن
factory	کارخانه	(see کردن)	کُن–
knife	کارد	shore	کِناره
worker	کارگِر	now	کُنون
member	کارمَند	up to now	تا کُنون
would that . . . !	کاش	present-day	کُنونی
plant	کاشتَن (کار–)	short	کوتاه
paper, letter	کاغِذ	small	کوچِک
enough	کافی	side-street	کوچه
complete	کامِل	child	کودَک
completely	کامِلاً	try	کوشیدَن
leap (year)	کَبیسه	star	کَوکَب (pl. کَواکِب)
book	کِتاب (pl. کُتُب)	mountain	کوه
bookshop	کِتابخانه	mountainous area	کوهِستان
bookseller	کِتابفُروش	salt desert	کَویر
dirty	کَثیف	that (conj.)	که
where?	کُجا	who?	که
which?	کُدام	who?	کی
do	کَردَن (کُن–)	when?	کَی
crore (500,000)	کُرور	kilogram	کیلو
Karim (male name)	کَریم		
person	کَس	**گ**	
kill	کُشتَن		
country	کِشوَر	bull, cow	گاو
draw, pull	کَشیدَن	place	گاه
shoemaker	کَفّاش	plaster	گَچ
shoe	کَفش	place, lay	گذاردَن

place, leave, allow	گذاشتن (گذار)
pass	گذشتن (گذر)
pass away	درگذشتن
apart from	گذشته از
expensive	گران
(see گشتن)	گرد –
spin (v. trans.) cause to turn	گردانیدن
hungry	گرسنه
victim, occupied	گرفتار
take, seize	گرفتن (گیر)
hot, warm	گرم
widespread	گسترده
opening	گشایش
be opened	گشایش یافتن
turn, become	گشتن (گرد–)
say, tell	گفتن (گو–)
conservation	گفتگو
mud	گِل
flower, rose	گُل
rose-garden	گلستان
lost	گم
appoint	گماشتن (گمار–)
unknown	گمنام
sin	گناه
wheat	گندم
(see گفتن)	گو–
ear	گوش
meat	گوشت
corner	گوشه
various	گوناگون
sort, kind	گونه
pearl	گوهر
perhaps	گویا
(see گرفتن)	گیر–
hold (n.)	گیر
get caught	گیر کردن
Gilan (Persian province)	گیلان

ل

necessary	لازم
clothes	لباس
aspect	لحاظ
tremble	لرزیدن
army	لشگر
London	لندن
favour	لطف
lame	لنگ
Lut (desert in S.E. Persia)	لوت
but	لیکن
tumbler	لیوان

م

we	ما
mother	مادر
Mazandaran (Persian province)	مازندران
motor-vehicle	ماشین
property; belonging to	مال
official	مأمور
remain	ماندن
Mani (Persian religious reformer)	مانی
Transoxania	ماورای النهر
moon, month	ماه
blessed	مبارک
beginner	مبتدی
afflicted	مبتلا
sum (of money)	مبلغ
based	مبنی
on the basis of	مبنی بر
foundation	مبنی (pl. مبانی)
sorry	متأسف
belligerent	متحارب
united	متحد
unite	متحد کردن
expert	متخصص

metre (measurement)	متر	director	مدیر
expected	مترقّب	city	مدینه (pl. مدُن)
joined	متّصل	sect	مذهب
join	متّصل ساختن	mirror	مرآت
numerous	متعدّد	regularly	مرتّباً
decomposing	متلاشی	time ('fois')	مرتبه
civilized	متمدّن	man	مرد
centralized	متمرکز	(pl. مردان = men, مردُم = people)	
requested	متمنّی	Mordad (5th month)	مرداد
appropriate	متناسب	die	مردَن (میر–)
engine	متور	written	مرقوم
suspected	متّهم	write	مرقوم فرمودن
like	مثل	centre	مرکز
triangular	مثلّث	central	مرکزی
allowed	مجاز	passing, course	مرور
punishment	مجازات	ill	مریض
neighbouring	مجاور	hospital	مریضخانه
nearness	مجاورت	crowded	مزدحم
splendid	مجلّل	farmland	مزرعه (pl. مزارع)
magazine	مجلّه	journey	مسافرت
equipped	مجهّز	travel (v.)	مسافرت کردن
unknown	مجهول	solid	مستحکم
needed	محتاج	employee	مستخدم
respected	محترم	counsellor	مستشار
deprived	محروم	independent	مستقلّ
student	محصّل (pl. . . . ین)	direct	مستقیم
firm	محکم	mosque	مسجد (pl. مساجد)
strengthen	محکم کردن	toothbrush	مسواک
Mohammad (male name)	محمّد	Christian	مسیحی
Mahmud (male name)	محمود	course, route	مسیر
obliteration	محو	responsible	مسئول
obliterate	محو کردن	witnessing	مشاهده
correspondent	مخبر	witness (v.)	مشاهده کردن
frightened	مخوف	constitution(al)	مشروطه
period, interval	مدّت	problem	مشکل
school	مدرسه	famous	مشهور
claimant	مدّعی	Egypt	مصر

catastrophic	مَصیبِت آوَر	national	مِلّی
disturbed	مُضطَرِب	possible	مُمکِن
corresponding to	مُطابِق	country	مَملِکَت
reading, study	مُطالَعه	I	مَن
press (printed)	مَطبوعات	resource	مَنبَع (مَنابِع .pl)
informed	مُطَّلِع	awaiting	مُنتَظِر
contemporary	مُعاصِر	awaited	مُنتَظَر
assistant	مُعاوِن	pulling	مُنجَرّ
temperate	مُعتَدِل	lead to	مُنجَرّ شُدن بِه
deposed	مَعزول	dissolved	مُنحَلّ
depose	مَعزول کَردن	house	مَنزِل (مَنازِل .pl)
known	مَعلوم	clerk	مُنشی
meaning	مَعنی	zone	مَنطَقه
shop	مَغازه	scene	مَنظَره
west	مَغرِب	reflected	مُنعَکِس
conquered	مَغلوب	profit	مَنفَعَت (مَنافِع .pl)
succumb	مَغلوب گَشتَن	hair	مو
Mongol(s), Mogul(s)	مُغول	treaty	مُوافَقَت
key	مِفتاح	effective	مُؤثِّر
inspector	مُفَتِّش	be effective	مُؤثِّر اُفتادَن
useful	مُفید	cause	موجِب
opposite	مُقابِل	dated	مُوَرَّخ
in exchange for	دَر مُقابِل	music	موسیقی
position	مَقام	successful	مُوَفَّق
arranged	مُقَرَّر	succeed	مُوَفَّق شُدَن
objective	مَقصَد	temporarily	مُوَقَّتاً
intention	مَقصود	occasion	مَوقِع
letter	مَکتوب (مَکاتیب .pl)	believer	مُؤمِن
surely; except	مَگَر	moonlit	مَهتابی
molla (priest)	مُلّا	Mehr (7th month)	مِهر
consideration	مُلاحَظه	Mehrabad (suburb of Tehran)	مِهرآباد
meeting	مُلاقات	kind (adj.)	مِهرَبان
meet	مُلاقات کَردن	important	مُهِمّ
nation	مِلَّت (مِلَل .pl)	hotel	مِهمانخانه
nationalism	مِلَّت پَرَستی	between	میان
king	مَلِک (مُلوک .pl)	Mithra (old Persian deity)	میتره
queen	مَلِکه	square (in town)	میدان

(see مُردن)	میر –	attribute	نِسبَت دادن
table	میز	sign	نِشان
possible	مُیَسَّر	show	نِشان دادن
inclination	مَیل	seat (v.)	نِشاندَن
like	مَیل داشتن	sit	نِشَستَن (نِشین)
birth	میلاد	wise counsel	نَصیحَتگَری
B.C.	قَبل آز میلاد	half	نِصف
A.D.	میلادی	sight	نَظَر (pl. آنظار)
million	میلیون	under the supervision of	تَحتِ نِظَرِ
fruit	میوه	equal, like	نَظیر
		exceptional	کَم نَظیر
	ن	person	نَفَر
		influence	نُفوذ
unclean	ناپاک	valuable	نَفیس
obliged; necessarily	ناچار	painter	نَقّاش
oblige	ناچار کردن	point	نُقطه (pl. نُقاط)
district	ناحِیه (pl. نَواحی)	point of view	نُقطهٔ نَظَر
ill	ناخوش	look (n.)	نِگاه
ignorant	نادان	keep; stop	نِگاه داشتن
Nader (male name)	نادِر	look (v.)	نِگاه کردن
suddenly	ناگاه	(see نمودن)	نَما –
name	نام	play (theat.)	نَمایِش
letter	نامه	play, script (theat.)	نَمایِشنامه
name (v.)	نامیدَن	representative	نَمایَنده
bread	نان	salt	نَمَک
lunch	ناهار	salt-cellar	نَمَکدان
grasping	نایِل	show (v.)	نَمودَن (نَما –)
achieve	نایِل شُدن به	new	نو
result	نَتیجه	play (instrument)	نَواختَن (نَواز –)
rescue (n.)	نِجات	ninety	نَوَد
rescue (v.)	نِجات دادن	nineteen	نوزدَه
carpenter	نَجّار	New Year's Day (March 21)	نوروز
no	نَخیر	writer	نویسَنده
first	نُخُست	Nushirvan (Sasanid king)	نوشیروان
near (prep.)	نَزد	kind, sort	نَوع (pl. آنواع)
near (adv. and prep.)	نَزدیک	servant	نوکَر
relatively	نِسبَةً	no	نَه

nine	نه	province, country, city; home	وِلایَت
nature	نِهاد	but	وَلی
bad-natured	بَدنِهاد	but	وَلیکِن
powerful	نیرومَند	ruined	ویران
also	نیز		
good	نیک		٥
half	نیم		
half (n.)	نیمه	Hejri, A.H. (Moslem calendar)	هِجری
		Achaemenian (first Persian dynasty)	هَخامَنِشی
	و	guidance	هِدایَت
		present, gift	هَدیه
and	وَ	each, every	هَر
entering	وارِد	never	هَرگِز
enter	وارِد شُدن	Hormozd (supreme, 'good' deity in Zoroastrian religion)	هُرمُزد
falling	واقِع		
in fact	دَرواقِع	thousand	هَزار
shoe-polish	واکس	eight	هَشت
polish (v.)	واکس کَردن	eighty	هَشتاد
grant	واگُذار کَردن	seven	هَفت
parents	والِدَین	seventy	هَفتاد
Valerian (Roman emperor)	والِریان	week	هَفته
existence	وُجود	seventeen	هِفدَه
exist	وُجود داشتَن	destruction	هَلاک
in spite of	باوُجود	be destroyed	هَلاک شُدن
in spite of the fact that	با وُجودیکه	also; even; together	هَم
terror	وَحشَت	already	هَم آکنون
blow (v. trans.)	وَزانیدَن	together	باهَم
minister	وَزیر (pl. وُزَرا)	fall to pieces, collapse	بِهَم خُوردن
middle (Arabic feminine form)	وُسطی	same	هَمان
means	وَسیله (pl. وَسایِل)	august	هُمایون
fatherland	وَطَن	Hamadan	هَمَدان
patriotism	وَطَن دوستی	together; companion	هَمراه
loyalty	وَفا	colleague	هَمکار
loyal	باوَفا	compatriot	هَموَطَن
disloyal	بی وَفا	all	هَمه
death	وَفات	always	هَمیشه
time ('temps')	وَقت (pl. آوقات)	same	هَمین
when	وَقتیکه		

just here	هَمینجا		ی
India	هِند (ـ وستان)	or	یا
academy	هُنَرِستان	ـ یاب (یافتَن see)	یاب ـ
time, moment	هِنگام	memory	یاد
yet, still	هَنوز	teach	یاد دادَن
air	هَوا	help (n.)	یاری
climate	آب و هَوا	eleven	یازدَه
aeroplane	هَواپِیما	find; gain (victory)	یافتَن (یاب ـ)
aeronautical; aviation	هَواپِیمائی	that is to say	یَعْنی
aerial	هَوائی	one	یَک
skill	هوش	one another	یَکدِیگَر
clever	باهوش	Sunday	یَکشَنبه
Hushang (male name)	هوشَنگ	day	یَوم (آیّام .pl)
eighteen	هِیجدَه	Greek	یونانی
any (with negative)	هیچ	countryside, summer resort	ییلاق
no one	هیچکَس		

I*

ENGLISH-PERSIAN VOCABULARY

N.B.—This vocabulary contains only those words used in the English–Persian exercises, and the Persian meanings given are only those appropriate to the uses required in those exercises.

A

Abbas	عَبّاس
abdication	إستِعفاء
able, be	تَوانِستَن (تَوان–)
above all	از هَمه بالاتر
accident	حادِثه (حَوادِث .pl)
Achaemenian	هَخامَنیشی
achieve	نایِل شُدَن به
achievement	شاهکار
A.D.	میلادی
administration	حُکومَت
adorn	آرایِش دادَن
affair	اَمر (اُمور .pl)
Afghan	آفغان
Afghanistan	آفغانِستان
after	بَعد از
again	باز، دوباره
again, once	بارِ دیگَر
age (era)	عَصر
ago	پیش
A.H.	هِجری
Akbar	اَکبَر
Alexander	إسکَندَر
Ali	عَلی
all	هَمه
already	هَم آکنون
also	هَم، نیز
although	اَگَرچه
among	ما بَین، از

anarchy	إغتِشاش
ancestor	جَدّ (آجداد .pl)
and	و
Anglo-	إنگلیسی
another	دیگَر، دیگَری، یَکی دیگَر
answer	جَواب
apparently	ظاهِراً
appear	ظُهور یافتَن
appearance	ظُهور
apple	سیب
Arabia	عَرَبِستان
Arabian	عَرَبی
Arabic	عَرَبی
Arabs (coll.)	عَرَب
Ardashir	اَردَشیر
army	لَشگَر
arts, fine	صَنایِع ظَریفه
Aryan	آریائی
as (in the form of)	بِرَسمِ
Ashkanian	آشکانی
Asia	آسیا
attack (n.)	حَمله (حَمَلات .pl)

B

bank	بانک
bazaar	بازار
B.C.	قَبل از میلاد
be	بودَن (باش–)
beautiful	زیبا

become	شُدَن (شَوَ–)	civilization	تَمَدُّن
begin	شُروع کَردن	civilized	مُتَمَدِّن
beginning	اِبتِدا	clean	پاک
beneath	زیر	climate	آب و هَوا
between	بَین	codify	تَدوین کَردَن
black	سیاه	collapse	بِهَم خُوردَن
book	کِتاب	come	آمَدَن (آ–)
boy	پِسَر	comfortable	راحَت
break up	بِهَم خُوردَن	commercial	تِجارَتی
bring	آوَردَن	company	شِرکَت
brother	بَرادَر	concession	اِمتیاز (اِمتیازات .pl)
build	ساختَن (ساز–)	consolidation	اِستِحکام
building	عِمارَت	constitution(al)	مَشروطه
but	آمّا، وَلی، لیکِن	contemporary	مُعاصِر
Buyids	آلِ بویه	continually	دائماً
by	به، با	correct	صَحیح
		corresponding to	مُطابِق
C		country	مَملِکَت، کِشوَر
caliph	خَلیفه (خُلَفا .pl)	course	مَسیر؛ مُرور
can (v.)	تَوانِستَن (تَوان–)	create	اِیجاد نَمودَن
capital	پایتَخت	crown	تاج
car	اُتومُبیل	culminate	خاتِمه یافتَن
careless	غافِل	cultural	فَرهَنگی
carry out	اِجرا کَردَن	culture	فَرهَنگ
catastrophic	مَصیبَت آوَر		
Caucasus	قَفقاز	**D**	
cave	غار	dangerous	خَطَرناک
central	مَرکَزی	Darius	داریوش
centralized	مُتَمَرکَز	daughter	دُختَر
centre	مَرکَز	day	روز، یَوم (اَیّام .pl)
century	قَرن (قُرون .pl)	dear	عَزیز
chair	صَندَلی	death	وَفات
cheap	آرزان	decisive	قاطِع
chieftain	سالار	defeat (v.)	شِکَستَن (شِکَن–)
child	بَچّه، کودَک	demand (n.)	تَقاضا
Christian	مَسیحی	democracy	دِموکراسی
city	شَهر	depose	مَعزول کَردَن

desert	بیابان	event	حادِثه (حَوادِث .pl)
die	مُردَن (میر–)	exist	وُجود داشتَن
difficult	سَخت	expand	تَوسِعه دادَن
dirty	کَثیف	expensive	گِران
discovery	اِکتِشاف	exploitation	اِستِثمار
district	ناحیه (نَواحی .pl)		
door	دَر	**F**	
drink	خوردَن		
drive	راندَن	fact, in	دَر واقِع
driver	رانَنده، شوفیر	factory	کارخانه
dry	خشکك	faith (religion)	دین
during	دَر	fall to pieces	بِهَم خوردَن
dynasty	خاندان	famous	مَشهور
		far	دور
E		Faridun	فَریدون
		farming	زِراعَت
earlier (adv.)	قَبل	farmland	مَزرَعه (مَزارِع .pl)
east	شَرق	father	پِدَر
easy	آسان	fault	تَقصیر
eat	خوردَن	feeling	حِسّ (اِحساسات .pl)
education	تَعلیم و تَربیَت	Ferdousi	فِردوسی
Egypt	مِصر	fight	جَنگ کَردَن
eight	هَشت	finally	آخِر، بِالآخِره
Elizabeth	اِلیزابِت	fine arts	صَنایِع ظَریفه
else, someone	کَسی دیگَر	first	اَوَّل، اَوَّلین، نُخُست
emperor	اِمپِراتور	first parts	آوایِل
empire	اِمپِراتوری	five	پَنج
encourage	تَشویق کَردَن	five-hundred-year	پانصَدساله
England	اِنگلِستان	for	بَرای
English	اِنگلیسی	force (v. trans.)	تَحمیل نَمودَن
Esma'il	اِسماعیل	found (v.)	تَأسیس کَردَن
establish	قِرار دادَن	foundation	آساس
established, be	بَرقِرار شُدَن	four	چَهار
establishment	تَشکیل	fresh	تازه
Europe	اُروپا	friend	دوست
European	اُروپائی	friendly	دوستانه
even	هَم	from	از
even though	آگَرچه	fruit	میوه

G

gain (find)	یافتَن (یاب –)
Ghazna	غَزنه
girl	دُختَر
glory	رَونَق
go	رَفتَن (رَو–)
gold	زَر
government	دَولَت، حُکومَت
gradually	رَفته رَفته
grant (v.)	واگُذار کَردَن
granting (n.)	اِعطا
great	بُزُرگ
Greek	یونانی
green	سَبز
guidance	هِدایَت

H

hair	مو
half (n.)	نیمه
Hamadan	هَمَدان
hand	دَست
Hasan	حَسَن
head	سَر
here	اینجا
history	تاریخ
Hosein	حُسَین
house	خانه، مَنزِل
how many?	چَند
humble (v.)	تَحقیر کَردَن
hundred	صَد
Hushang	هوشَنگ

I

I	مَن
idea	عَقیده (عَقایِد .pl)
if	اَگَر
impact	بَرخُورد

importance	اَهَمّیَّت
important	مُهِمّ
in	دَر، تو
internal	داخِلی
into	دَر، به
inaugurate	اِفتِتاح نَمودَن
independent	مُستَقِلّ
India	هِند (– وِستان)
Indus river	رودِ سِند
industrial	صَنعَتی
influence	نُفوذ
ink	جَوهَر
instruction	دَستور (دَستورات .pl)
interrupted, be	قَطع شُدَن
interval	مُدَّت
invasion	حَمله (حَمَلات .pl)
Iraq	عِراق
irrigation	آبیاری
Isfahan	اِصفَهان
Islam	اِسلام
Islamic	اِسلامی

J

just (righteous)	عادِل

K

Karim	کَریم
Khan	خان
Khorasan	خُراسان
king	پادشاه
knife	کارد
knock at	زَدَن (زَن –)
known	مَعلوم

L

land	زَمین
language	زَبان
large	بُزُرگ

last (adj.)	آخِرین
last parts	آواخِر
law	قانون (قَوانین pl.)
lay	گذاردَن
lead to	مُنجَرّشُدَن به
lesson	دَرس
life	زَندَگی
like	مِثل
limit	حَدّ (حُدود pl.)
literature	آدَبیات
live	زیستَن (زی–)
lofty	عالی
long years	سالیانِ دَراز
lose	از دَست دادَن
lunar	قَمَری

M

madam	خانُم
Mahmud	مَحمود
make	ساختَن (ساز–)
man	مَرد (مَردان، مَردُم pl.)
manager	رَئیس
Mani	مانی
manifested, be	بُروز شُدَن
many	خَیلی، بِسیار، زِیاد
means	وَسیله (وَسایل pl.)
means of, by	تَوَسُّطِ
meat	گوشت
mention	ذِکر کَردَن
Mesopotamia	عِراق
Middle Ages	قُرونِ وُسطی
middle parts	آواسِط
modernization	تَجَدُّد
Mogul	مُغول
Mohammad	مُحَمَّد
monarch	سُلطان
Mongols	مُغول

more	بیشتَر، بیش
mosque	مَسجِد (مَساجِد pl.)
mother	مادَر
motor-car	اُتومبیل
motor-vehicle	ماشین
much	خَیلی، بِسیار، زِیاد
must	بایِستَن (با–)

N

Nader	نادِر
name (n.)	اِسم
name, make one's	شُهرَت یافتَن
nation	مِلَّت (مِلَل pl.)
national	مِلّی
nationalism	مِلَّت پَرَستی
natural	طَبیعی
near (adj. and prep.)	نَزدیک
(prep.)	پیش، نَزد
necessary, be	بایِستَن (با–)
neither one	هیچیک
new	نَو، تازه، جَدید
news	خَبَر (آخبار pl.)
next (adv., conj.)	سِپَس
nine	نُه
nineteen	نوزدَه
no (interj.)	نَه، نَخَیر، خَیر
no (adj.)	هیچ
north	شِمال
not (with verb)	نَه
numerous	مُتَعَدِّد
Nushirvan	نوشیرواَن

O

obliterate	مَحوکَردَن
occupy	اِشغال کَردَن، تَصَرُّف کَردَن
of: use ezafe	
old (things)	قَدیم

on	روی، بتر، ستر
once again	بار دیگر
one	یک، یکی
only	فقط
open (adj.)	باز
or	یا
other	دیگر
Ottoman	عثمانی
overthrow	سرنگون کردن

P

Pahlavi	پهلوی
painter	نقّاش
palace	کاخ
Papakan	پاپکان
paper	کاغذ
part	قسمت
part of, on the	از طرف
Parthian	پارت (پارتها pl.)
parts, first	اوایل
parts, middle	اواسط
parts, last	اواخیر
Parvin	پروین
patriotism	وطن دوستی
peaceful	صلح آمیز
pen	قلم
people	مردم
period	دوره، مدّت
Persepolis	تخت جمشید
Persia	ایران
Persian	ایرانی
person	کس، شخص (اشخاص pl.)
personality	شخصیت (. . . ها pl.)
pieces, fall to	بهم خوردن
place (v.)	گذاشتن (گذار-)، گذاردن
plateau	فلات
pleased	راضی

poet	شاعر (شعرا pl.)
point of view	نقطهٔ نظر
policeman	پاسبان
popular	عوام پسند
possible	ممکن، میسّر
post office	پستخانه
pour out (intr.)	بیرون ریختن
power	قدرت
powerful	نیرومند
prehistoric	قبل از تاریخ
present	حاضر
pretty	خوشگل
prevalent	شایع
problem	مشکل
programme	برنامه
progress	ترقّی
prophet	پیغمبر

Q

Qajar	قاجار
queen	ملکه
question	سؤال (. . . ات pl.)

R

read	خواندن
ready	حاضر
red	سرخ
reform	اصلاح
reign (n.)	سلطنت
reign (v.)	سلطنت کردن
reins	زمام
reject	ردّ کردن
relation	رابطه (روابط pl.)
religion	دین
religious leader	روحانی (. . . ین pl.)
repeated, be	تکرار شدن
resource	منبع (منابع pl.)

restore	قرار گذاشتَن	sharp	تیز
result, as a	دَر نتیجه	Shi'a	شیعه
revive	قوَّت دادَن	Shiraz	شیراز
Reza	رضا	shore	کِناره
rich (fertile)	حاصلخیز	short	کوتاه
rival	رَقیب (pl. رُقَبا)	show	نَمودَن (نَما–)
Roman	رومی	sides, two	طَرَفَین
royal	شاهی، شاهَنشاهی	simple	ساده
Rudaki	رودَکی	sincere	صَمیمانه
rule (n.)	حُکومَت	sir	آقا
rule (v.)	حُکومَت کَردَن	sister	خواهَر
Russia	روسیه	sit	نِشَستَن (نِشین–)
Russian	روسی	six	شِش
		sleep (n.)	خواب
S		small	کوچِک
Safavid	صَفَوی	snow	بَرف
Safidrud	سَفیدرود	society	اِجتِماع
Samanids	آل سامان	solar	شَمسی
same	هَمین، هَمان	Soleiman	سُلَیمان
same time, at the	دَر عَینِ حال	someone else	کَسی دیگَر
Sasanid	ساسانی	son	پِسَر
say	گُفتَن (گو–)	sour	تُرش
scheme	طَرح	south (n.)	جُنوب
sea	دَریا	south (adj.)	جُنوبی
second	دوُّم، دوُیُم	space of, in the	دَر ظَرفِ
sect	مَذهَب	spite of, in	با وُجود
see	دیدَن (بین–)	spread (intr.)	رَواج یافتَن
seize	گِرِفتَن (گیر–)	stability	ثَبات
self	خوُد، خویش	state	دَولَت (pl. دوُل)
Seljuq	سَلجوق	still	هَنوز
send	فِرِستادَن (فِرِست–)	strange	غَریب
sequence	رِشته	street	خیابان
seven	هَفت	strengthen	مُحکَم کَردَن
seventy	هَفتاد	strike	زَدَن (زَن–)
Shah	شاه	strong	قَوی
Shapur	شاپور	student	مُحَصِّل (pl. . . . ین)
share	سَهم	submerged, be	غَرق شُدَن

succeed	مُوَفَّق شُدَن	throne	تَخت
successor	جانِشین	time ('temps')	وَقت، زَمان
succumb	مَغلوب گَشتَن	time (period)	مُدَّت
suddenly	ناگاه	to	به
sultan	سُلطان	today	اِمروز
surface	سَطح	together	باهَم، هَمراه
Susa	شوش	town	شَهر
sweet	شیرین	Transoxania	ماوَرَایَ النَّهر
sweets	شیرینی	travel (v.)	مُسا فَرَت کَردَن
Syria	سوریه	tree	دَرَخت
		tribe	ایل (ایلات .pl)
T		true	صحیح
table	میز	Turkish	تُرکی
take	گِرِفتَن (گیر–)	turn into	گَشتَن (گَرد–) به
take away	بُردَن (بَر–)	twelve	دَوازدَه
Tamerlane	تیمور لَنگ	twenty	بیست
tea	چای	two	دُو
teach	آموختَن (آموز–)	two hundred	دَویست
technique	أُسلوب (أَساییب .pl)	two sides	طَرَفَین
Tehran	تِهران		
tell	گُفتَن (گو–)	**U**	
ten	دَه	under	زیر، تَحت
than	اَز	unite	مُتَّحِد کَردَن
that (conj.)	که	unity	اِتِّحاد
that (pron.)	آن		
there	آنجا	**V**	
there is	هَست	Valerian	والِریان
these	این، اینها	vehicle	ماشین
third	سِیُّم	very	خَیلی، بِسیار
thirteen	سیزدَه	very much	خَیلی، بِسیار
thirty	سی	victory	پیروزی
this	این	vigorous	شَدید
those	آن، آنها		
though	اَگَرچه	**W**	
thousand	هَزار	war	جَنگ
three	سه	we	ما
three hundred	سیصَد	western	غَربی

what?	چه		

Y

which?	کدام	year	سال
who?	کی، که	years, long	سالیان دراز
whole	تمام	yellow	زرد
widely	زیاد	yes	بلی
winter	زمِستان	young	جوان
with	با، به		
within	دَر ظَرف	**Z**	
witness (v.)	مُشاهَده کردَن	Zand	زَند
work (n.)	کار	zenith	اوج
work (v.)	کار کردَن	Zoroaster	زَردُشت
world (adj.)	جَهانی	Zoroastrian	زَردُشتی

INDEX

(References are to paragraphs)